THE
LITTLE
HISTORY
OF
DERBYSHIRE

THE
LITTLE
HISTORY
OF
DERBYSHIRE

JULIA A. HICKEY

The
History
Press

First published 2024

The History Press
97 St George's Place, Cheltenham,
Gloucestershire, GL50 3QB
www.thehistorypress.co.uk

British Library Cataloguing in Publication Data.
A catalogue record for this book is available from the British Library.

ISBN 978 1 80399 415 4

Typesetting and origination by The History Press.
Printed and bound in Great Britain by TJ Books Limited, Padstow, Cornwall.

Trees for Life

CONTENTS

ABOUT THE AUTHOR

Julia Hickey's interest in the history of Derbyshire began more than twenty-five years ago when she first moved to the Peak District. She has worked in a variety of educational settings including Sheffield Hallam University and the Workers' Educational Association, where she drew on Derbyshire's rich and diverse past as a focus for teaching. She is currently a freelance tutor and blogger at thehistoryjar.com.

Julia has written five history books as well as short stories for magazines that often draw their inspiration from her surroundings. Julia loves exploring old churches, castles and museums. She enjoys walking and photographing Derbyshire's spectacular views as well as discovering unexpected elements of the landscape, such as the 1,500 or so discarded millstones left where they were hewn from the rock.

1

THE BEGINNING OF DERBYSHIRE

About 340 million years ago, in an era known as the Carboniferous period, Derbyshire was covered by a warm, shallow sea and bordered by a series of coral reefs, beyond which lay deep water. The clear tropical expanse was teeming with life, including sharks and dolphins. Shelled creatures called brachiopods with two hinged shells, bivalve molluscs and forests of five-armed crinoids resembling modern sea urchins, covered the seabed. The latter are sometimes called sea lilies because their fossilised remains look more like plants than animals. When the marine life died, their remains (rich in calcium carbonate) drifted to the seabed, built up over millennia, and compacted to form limestone.

From time to time, volcanoes on the seabed south-west of modern Matlock and in the area around Tideswell exploded, ejecting ash and lava that solidified rapidly to create hard igneous rocks between the beds of softer limestone. Magma (molten rock), rich in minerals, forced its way into gaps and fissures in the sedimentary layers that crystalised as it cooled, forming veins of lead, copper, fluorspar and Blue John, among more than 100 mineral types to be found in Derbyshire.

Conditions changed very gradually but the seabed was forever altering. Great rivers flowed south from mountains pushed up in the north during the earlier Devonian geological period. The water slowed when it reached the shallows, creating a landscape of braided deltas. The currents were no longer able to carry their load of sediment and other materials when they reached the outer limits of the shallow sea. The deposits left on the reef boundaries created layers of millstone grit and shale on top of limestone in the region that would become Derbyshire's Peak District. Finer silts and sediments continued on their journey into the deep seas to the east and west, beyond the reefs.

As the deltas expanded, they created a densely vegetated swamp. Trees and ferns thrived. When they died and rotted, they in turn became compressed, the land subsided, and the sea reclaimed the area as the cycle repeated itself, creating bands of compacted mud, clay and sandstones. Transformed plant remains formed a layer known as the Coal Measures running through the north-east of Derbyshire southwards to the Amber Valley, Erewash and into the Trent Valley.

Water continued to ebb and flow, sculpting the earth as it moved. The land buckled under enormous pressures and pushed up bands of rock laid down in earlier periods into a geological formation known as the Derbyshire Dome. The exposed layers were subject to the forces of wind, rain and ice

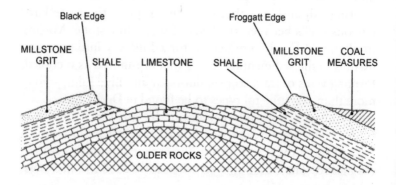

that scoured away the sandstones, millstone grits and shale to create a plateau and to reveal the oldest limestone deposits of the modern White Peak, extending from Wirksworth in the south to Castleton in the north. Despite the erosion, the uplands in this area are between 250m and 400m above sea level today. The more elevated gritstones and shales are the foundations of the Dark Peak in the north-west of the county, of which Kinder Scout, 624m above sea level, is a part. The exposed gritstone that lay to either side of the Derbyshire Dome formed steep cliffs known locally as 'edges', including Stanage Edge, Curbar Edge, Gardom's and Froggatt Edge to the east, and in the west the escarpment known as the Roaches.

Around 2.4 million years ago the first of a succession of Ice Ages covered the region with a sheet of ice hundreds of metres thick, carving out valleys and scouring the uplands. The ice advanced and retreated on at least four occasions as the climate cooled and then warmed again. In the south of Derbyshire, a landscape created from layers of sediment was covered by fertile glacial deposits carried south by ice sheets and then left behind as they retreated. Elsewhere, the ice left huge boulders, known as erratics, carried long distances from their source areas. Several of these can be found on the edge of Stanton Moor near Bakewell, including the Cat Stone and the Three Ships, found at Birchen Edge near Baslow.

Water draining from the uplands eroded the blankets of glacial sediment and cut through the sandstone beneath to create gently rolling hills. Today the landscape to the south-west of

Derbyshire is characterised by the River Dove and pasture that extends across its wide valley. Further north, as the ice melted, rivers created valleys before disappearing underground through cracks and fissures, dissolving the limestone as it flowed, forming caves and caverns. Some dales still have streams running through them, but others are dry or seasonal.

A raging torrent of meltwater, which would become the River Derwent, moulded the gritstone edges with its erosive force before slicing through shale and mudstone deposits to create a wide valley. The river wound south, collecting water from within its catchment of smaller rivers, streams and channels until it met with the River Trent not far south-east of Derby. The process of water erosion and deposition created bands of undulating sand and mudstones on their floodplains. Over time, the water deposited sand and gravel, forming deep terraces on either side of the rivers to create a light loam-based soil that lends itself to farming. The lowlands remain an unambiguous contrast to the north-west of Derbyshire that form part of the chain of Pennine Hills described as the 'backbone of England'.

EARLY DERBYSHIRE INHABITANTS

Between 55,000 and 40,000 years ago the region looked more like Siberian grassland tundra than the landscape of today. Fossil remains tell us that herds of woolly mammoth, rhinos, deer and bison came in search of food. Britain was not yet an island. It was joined by a wide land bridge to Europe. Sea levels were as much as 120m lower than they are today because water was locked into the ice sheets. The herds were followed by hyenas, lions and wolves.

Small groups of Neanderthal people advanced north in search of food and shelter from near-Arctic conditions. Their population was small and almost all traces of them have been

obliterated by repeated glaciation. Neanderthals, who proceeded modern *Homo sapiens*, were physically adapted to cold environments. They made temporary homes in upland areas in Derbyshire's brief summers. Archaeological evidence shows that they visited Creswell Crags and other caves. When winter tightened its grip and the herds migrated south along the Trent Valley in search of fresh grazing, the men and women who hunted them followed. On occasion, plummeting temperatures and sheets of ice up to a mile thick in places made Derbyshire far too inhospitable for anything to flourish.

The nomadic population returned whenever the ice retreated. They camped near rivers or on hills overlooking valleys. Evidence of windbreaks, hearths and stone tools have been found at Wetton Mill and Broomhead Moor in the Peak District. Families revisited the same sites over a long period of time, following established seasonal routes to places they knew to be rich in wildlife, berries and edible plants. Other groups found shelter in the limestone cave systems in the Manifold Valley; at Ravensdale, between Wardlow and Cressbrook, where a 40,000-year-old flint scraper was discovered; and at Creswell Crags in the north-east of modern-day Derbyshire, on the border with Nottinghamshire.

The men and women who lived at Creswell and other cave systems hunted their prey at close range with spears before returning to their caves or camps, where they butchered the meat in the light of fires built for warmth and to drive off animals. Bears, lions and hyenas presented a danger, but their skins provided clothing and blankets while their teeth and claws were worn as decoration. The people who lived in Robin Hood Cave at Creswell Crags made chopping and scraping tools from quartzite, or chert, a local stone harder than flint. Inhabitants of the crags crafted tools from bones and antlers as well as knapping flint from cores they carried with them into Derbyshire to make hand axes, scrapers and arrow heads.

Evidence for Neanderthal occupation anywhere stops about 36,000 years ago. It is unclear why the species became extinct. It has been suggested that they could not adapt to the warming climate at the end of the last Ice Age. More significantly, perhaps, their disappearance from the archaeological record coincides with the arrival of *Homo sapiens* in Europe from Africa. It is uncertain whether early modern humans brought new diseases with them or if the two groups competed for limited resources.

Homo sapiens migrants began to use the caves that the Neanderthal inhabited at Creswell and elsewhere about 29,000 years ago. Excavations have uncovered spear heads, scrapers, knives, bone needles, awls and borers. Hunters started using bows and arrows for the first time. The herds of woolly mammoth and rhinoceros had not returned as the ice retreated. Instead, deer, bison and smaller mammals including hare and lemming were on the menu. Around 12,500 years ago, at Robin Hood's Cave, someone spent time carefully engraving a wild horse's head onto a piece of bone. Another engraving, on a piece of reindeer rib, found in Pin Hole Cave also at Creswell, depicts what appears to be a human wearing a mask and holding a bow. Whoever lived in the row of limestone caves also created Britain's only known cave art, depicting the herds of bison, horse and deer that roamed the land around Creswell as well as a bird, carved into the ceiling, with a long, curved beak like an ibis.

Derbyshire is rich in prehistoric rock art. Its existence and range of sites where it may be found helps to show that as the climate became more temperate, migrant hunters extended their range to the north-west and north-east of Derbyshire. Artists carved patterns into rock surfaces that include rings, spirals, arcs, zigzags and hollows known as 'cups'. The shapes are difficult to date as some of the designs are thought to have originated in the later Bronze Age. It is impossible to know what the symbols may have meant. Their outdoor location and the use of horizontal surfaces for the decoration suggests some astronomical significance. A carved boulder at Ashover dates from between 3,000 and 6,000 years ago, although the best-known rock art can be found at Gardom's Edge.

As the planet warmed, the climate became milder and wetter and the ice sheets continued their retreat, releasing water as they melted. Sea levels rose, filling the area of the North Sea and the Channel with water. Britain became an island. Around 4,000 BC men and women began to take up permanent residence in Derbyshire, which was almost completely covered in forest.

Most people chose to live in places that were good vantage points for hunting the herds of deer and wild pig that roamed the hills. They caught birds and fish and also gathered crab apples, hazel nuts, edible berries and plants. The hunters used arrow tips made from shards of triangular flint or chert called microliths that were set in rows with resin. They began to clear the forest with burning so that they could catch the game that came to feed on new growth. As well as making hunting more predictable, it also had the effect of eroding the thin upland soil. When the weather became wetter, the ground became waterlogged and moorland peat started to form.

LISMORE FIELDS AND DERBYSHIRE'S FIRST FARMERS

One group made their home near the River Wye at Lismore Fields, Buxton. It is described as one of the most important Neolithic settlements so far found in Britain. Excavation revealed post holes and timber floors that were all that remained of two neolithic longhouses, as well as a later Mesolithic roundhouse. The site also contained stone tools, worked flint and pottery.

The Lismore Pot, a shouldered pot which is about 5,500 years old, is one of the oldest pots ever discovered in Britain. Analysis of residue attached to the inside of the bowl and other pottery shards found at the site showed that the people who lived at Lismore reared cattle for meat and for milk, ate honey taken from wild bees, and gathered apples.

Cereal stores were also discovered. Archaeologists believe that Lismore Fields could be the site of the earliest cereal farming yet discovered in the whole country. Analysis of food residues also indicated that Lismore's population ate emmer wheat. Emmer wheat is a wild grass that was gathered and cooked as a porridge. Farming is thought to have been introduced to Britain in around 4000 BC. It is also possible that, rather than growing it themselves, the wheat was being gathered from the wild, or even that it was being traded along a network that extended across the seas.

In about 3500 BC the hunters and gathers who lived in Britain began to change their habits. There were still large numbers of wild animals roaming Derbyshire's forests, including aurochs and deer, but the larger animals of earlier times were replaced by wild boar, foxes, hares, squirrel, beavers, bears and wolves. As well as hunting and gathering, the people of Derbyshire started to farm the land. They wanted to keep cattle and to help edible herbaceous plants and roots to grow. They were already clearing trees to encourage herds of deer to graze on new growth to ensure good hunting, but now they began to clear more trees, using polished stone axes, to create fields for pasture and for crops.

HIGHS AND LOWS

At about the same time that the people who lived in Derbyshire began to farm, they also began to build barrows on top of hills and ridges where they buried their dead. Place names ending in 'Low' in Derbyshire often indicate the site of burials or cairns. In total, there are more than 500 barrows across the region, dating mainly from the Neolithic period to the Bronze Age. The word comes from the Old English '*hlaw*', which means a rounded hill. In Derbyshire these summits are the high points upon which burial mounds were often built and which still dominate the landscape today.

The first burial chambers were chambered tombs formed from immense stone slabs and lengths of dry stone walling incorporating a central passageway to the burial chambers. The structures were covered with a mound of earth, but they were not closed once an interment took place. People could access the corridor through a narrow stone-lined entrance so that they could revisit the bodies of their ancestors. There is evidence that they rearranged or even removed the bones on occasion. Many generations might be buried in one tomb or their cremated remains placed there.

The cairns were a reminder that the ancestors were never far away. They may also have made a statement about land-ownership and belonging. Minninglow is Derbyshire's largest tomb and can be seen for many miles. The tree-capped hill dominates the horizon between Parwich and Elton. It began as a small mound but developed into a long mound with four or more burial chambers. Later still, it was enlarged again with the addition of two bowl barrows. These new earthworks and the addition of an encircling dry stone wall created a huge circular mound, approximately 40m in diameter. Like most of the other burial mounds in the Peak District, it demonstrates evidence of repeated use at different times. Excavation revealed Roman pottery and coins as well as fragments of earlier bones.

In common with most of the barrows in the Peak District, it was excavated during the Victorian Period by Thomas Bateman, who discovered that its contents had been robbed by earlier treasure hunters.

THE BARROW KNIGHT

Thomas Bateman, born in 1821 in Rowsley near Bakewell, was raised after his father's death, when Thomas was 14, by his grandfather at Middleton Hall in Middleton-by-Youlgreave. He became enthralled by the number of burial mounds that dotted the Peak District and by his grandfather's antiquarian collection of finds and books.

As a young man Bateman was introduced to archaeological excavation when a medieval church in Bakewell was demolished. In 1844 he joined in the excavation of prehistoric graves in Kent supervised by the British Archaeological Association. The following year, Bateman excavated thirty-eight barrows in Derbyshire and Staffordshire, earning the nickname 'The Barrow Knight'. During his life he excavated more than 200 burial mounds and kept records of his work, writing two books, which included beautiful illustrations of the finds that he excavated. His methods, although disapproved of today for their speed and use of labourers without formal archaeological training, were good for the time. He kept accounts of what he was excavating, unlike many others who dug into Derbyshire's ancient barrows and left no record of what they found. He also left a brass token labelled 'T. Bateman' in place of the finds he removed and kept in his collection at his home.

He died, aged 39, at Middleton-by-Youlgreave and was buried, according to his wishes, in a field behind the chapel rather than in the local churchyard. His tomb includes a stone replica of a Bronze Age collared urn like the ones he unearthed from Derbyshire's barrows.

THE BRONZE AGE (C. 2300 BC–800 BC)

A new group of settlers, possibly originating from the area of modern Spain, began to spread across northern Europe. The Beaker people, named after the drinking vessel associated with archaeological finds where they lived and which were often buried with their dead, arrived in Derbyshire around 4,500 years ago but populations continued to be concentrated in the upland areas. People adopted new cultural practices as the two groups merged.

At about the same time as the Beaker people became a part of Derbyshire's DNA, its inhabitants began to build henges constructed from a stone circle surrounded by a massive ditch and bank. They built one at Arbor Low, south-west of Bakewell, and another about 10 miles to the north-west at Dove Holes called the Bull Ring. Both lie on the same prehistoric trackway, suggesting ideal meeting points for both ritual and for trade.

THE STONEHENGE OF THE NORTH

The most important henge in Derbyshire is at Arbor Low. It sits on an exposed limestone ridge 373m above sea level close to Gib Hill long barrow. The burial cairn, one of the few in the Peak District not to be round, was already old when work on the henge first began. Excavations in 1901 showed that Arbor Low's 3m-deep outer ditch was dug with the aid of antler tine picks and shovels made from ox bone. As the channel was quarried, other labourers transported the soil to a bank inside the ditch with wicker baskets. It probably took several years and an entire community's labour to complete.

An inner earth bank, when Arbor Low was first built, stood 3m high and 8–10m wide. The bank and ditch are interrupted by two entrances; one to the north-west and the second to the south-east. Inside the bank there was a 43m-wide circle of fifty lime stones, now flattened and eroded. There is also a small group of four fallen stones at the middle of the ring called a 'cove'. Archaeologists believe that this confined space, hidden from view by the stones that enclosed it, was where religious rituals or ceremonies took place, out of sight of the majority of the people who gathered at the henge.

It has been argued that the location of the henge is significant to the rising of the midwinter sun. It is also plausible that it might have some relation to the setting of a full moon at midwinter and in midsummer. Whatever the possible associations, astronomical alignments and cultural significance, it is certain that people came together from across the uplands and perhaps beyond to celebrate special times of the year.

BRONZE AGE INDUSTRY

The Beaker people knew how to work metals. Excavation of a burial chamber at Staker Hill near Buxton revealed a skeleton adorned with bronze ear clips, while another barrow at Haddon, near Bakewell, yielded a bronze awl. At first smiths used copper, but they soon learned to make bronze, which is an alloy of copper and tin. Bronze tools and weapons began to appear more frequently, although they remained luxury items used by elite members of society. Most people continued to use stone tools. Barbed and tanged arrow heads and polished axeheads have been found across Derbyshire dating from this period.

At first, the smiths who created new metal tools mimicked earlier stone ones, but gradually the metal workers improved upon the designs they created. Flat axes were cast by pouring molten metal alloys into simple, single, flat stone moulds. Later, axes were cast using two-part moulds, and by the end of the Bronze Age smiths were able to produce an axe head with a hollow socket at its base so that a wooden haft could be inserted.

Underground, the county's first mining industry was beginning to take shape. Miners at Ecton Hill, to the south-west beyond the Manifold Valley near Warslow, extracted copper and lead ore with bone and red deer antler picks, as well as hammer stones, following mineral veins uphill by means of shallow drifts.

BRONZE AGE BURIALS

Burial practices had changed. Communal mounds fell out of use. Many of the smaller mounds that dot high ground in the Peak District originate from the Bronze Age. Cairn builders began to create stone boxes known as 'cists' at the base of the tomb, where a single body or urn containing cremated remains was placed carefully. Mounds were enlarged if required or new mounds created. They cluster together in the landscape, often near other prehistoric monuments.

Two new circular burial mounds were superimposed on the older landscape at Arbor Low and Gibb's Hill, making it more prominent in the landscape. A burial mound was created from the bank at Arbor Low with a small internal stone chamber containing food pots, a bronze pin and a cremation. At Beeley Moor, near Chatsworth, an area inhabited throughout the Bronze Age, there are three joined mounds that are part of a system of burials, stone circles and field structures. The best known is Hob Hurst's House at Harland Edge, but its rectangular shape has led to some speculation that it might be Iron rather than Bronze Age. When Bateman excavated it in 1853, he found evidence of a cremation. Pots were often placed with the dead or they were buried as containers for cremated remains. As in earlier times, it is thought that the burial mounds reinforced a connection to the land for the living where their ancestors were buried.

Small stone circles sprouted on the moorland uplands. The circles are often associated with urns containing cremation burials. They could have been built by extended families rather than entire communities. The Wet Withens stone circle, built on a rubble bank on Eyam Moor, looks towards Higger Tor. The stones, which are up to a metre tall, are almost invisible during the summer months because of the long grasses and heathers. More accessible, the Nine Ladies on Stanton Moor contains a ring of stones, each upright and less than a metre high. According to legend, the nine standing stones on Stanton Moor and their accompanying 'King Stone' were revellers petrified by an outraged priest when he caught them dancing on Sunday. In reality, the stones are part of a more complicated network of standing stones and prehistoric circles that cover the moor.

On a clear day the hill at Minninglow with its Neolithic and Bronze Age tombs can be seen across the area, joining communities together as well as marking boundaries.

A LEGENDARY TOWN

Potential Bronze Age settlements have been identified to the north-east of Derbyshire near Dronfield, and at Totley Moor near Sheffield. Legends also persist about a sunken town at Leash Fen, 305m above sea level between Chesterfield and Baslow. Today the area is a boggy stretch of heather and gorse. A well-known local rhyme states:

> When Chesterfield was gorse and broom
> Leash Fen was a market town;
> Now Chesterfield is a market town,
> Leash Fen is but gorse and broom.

Occasionally pieces of pottery and worked oak are excavated during drainage work, suggesting that there is some truth to the story.

A CHANGE IN WEATHER

Botanical evidence shows that life became more difficult for Derbyshire's Bronze Age inhabitants as the climate became increasingly wet and unpredictable. Much of the Stone and Bronze Age archaeology of the Peak District lies beneath peat, which forms in waterlogged conditions. Farmers, like those who lived at Leash Fen, were no longer able to grow their arable crops in the highest upland areas. It is also possible that the shallow soils associated with the limestone plateau and gritstone edges was exhausted after centuries of cultivation.

As the weather continued to deteriorate, crops failed and the soil became unworkable, the Peak District's climate refugees sought out new land to call their own and the peat blanketed once thriving prehistoric settlements. Some communities moved from the uplands to lowland river valleys, where they deforested the land and began to rebuild their lives.

IRON AGE DERBYSHIRE (800 BC TO AD 50)

Immigrants from Western Europe travelled north and west along the river routes that heralded the arrival of earlier settlers into Derbyshire, joining the existing population in the valleys and uplands. Genome sequencing shows that they intermarried with the people who were already here and shared their new iron working skills. At Burbage Brook, near Hathersage, evidence of iron smelting has been uncovered. As well as weapons, iron ploughshares meant that more land could be planted.

People often continued to live as they had done for generations, in timber roundhouses with their doors facing south-east to benefit from natural light and warmth. They settled in the Trent Valley, dividing the land into field systems with ditches and paddocks. In the upland areas, fields were laboriously cleared of stone so that more land could be cultivated. Stones were left in small piles or along the edge of the field boundaries. At Big Moor, an enterprising family used stone to foot the walls of their home.

Excavation at Ravencliff Cave in Cressbrook Dale unearthed Neolithic axe blades and flint scrapers, as well as pottery from the Iron Age. Harborough Rocks, near the village of Brassington, sits 379m above sea level. It has provided a home for people since the Ice Age. Excavation in 1889 by J. Ward and C. Gregory uncovered potsherds, charcoal and animal bone. At the time it was concluded that the finds belonged to the Iron Age, a view that was confirmed by twentieth-century excavations and analysis of finds.

As the population grew, more land was cleared and people formed themselves into tribes to defend their territories. The earliest written evidence of the so-called Ancient Britons who spoke a Celtic language is from Greco-Roman writers, who described tribal groups tied together by language, culture and religion. The Brigantes, which translates to 'the high ones', were the largest and most powerful tribe in the north of England. They held the area north of Derby. Some of the lowland region to the south of the county was held by the Corieltauvi or Coritani, who ruled the East Midlands. Control of the border zone between the two tribes shifted over time.

THE SHIVERING MOUNTAIN, IRON AGE HILLFORTS AND MURDER IN THE PEAK DISTRICT

The increased size of the population, changing climate and lack of food led to increased need for protection as family groups competed for the available resources. Tribes invested in the labour and time necessary for the construction of hilltop retreats. Hill forts, with their circuits of banks and ditches placed on hill tops and ridges, prominent Iron Age monuments, make dramatic statements echoing down the centuries about the power of the Brigantes in Derbyshire.

Mam Tor, or the 'Shivering Mountain' because of the shale landslides on its eastern side, is near Castleton. The site has been the location of human activity since prehistoric times. Flints and a polished stone axe have been found here, as well as a late Bronze Age socketed axe head. The hill fort, dominating the landscape from the top of a 517m summit, is the largest fort in the Peak District, with a ditch and ramparts standing 7–9m high, enclosing approximately 16 acres of ground with two gateways. When it was excavated in 1965, post hole foundations were discovered for 100 small platforms on which huts were built, showing that a thriving village grew up around two Bronze Age bowl barrows.

Iron Age forts may have had a range of other purposes apart from defensive ones, including the protection of flocks from theft; as summer grazing deserted during the winter months; for rituals; and as meeting places. Ten miles to the south-west of Mam Tor, Castle Naze, at Combs Moss near

Chapel-en-le-Frith, is a triangular hill fort on a promontory protected by a deep ditch and double ramparts nearly 168m long on one side, and by steep slopes on its other two sides. On a clear day it's possible to see for miles, but during the winter months it is a wild and inhospitable place.

There are several smaller hill forts, or defensive structures, scattered across the Peak District, which would have provided little security in the event of a sustained attack. Ball's Cross near Bakewell, Carl Wark near Burbage, and Castle Ring on Harthill Moor are all described as forts. Castle Ring, the smallest in the region, encloses only ¾ acre on the crest of a hill. It was at best a short-term refuge, but it had two banks and a ditch that create its oval structure.

Carl Wark, which is boulder strewn, is shaped by a rocky escarpment, its embankment reinforced with stone blocks to form an enclosure with a gateway. Besides not offering any-where for shelter, it is overlooked by Higger Tor to the north. There is nothing else like it in the north of England and it is regarded as being of national importance. No one is absolutely certain when it was built. It may be Neolithic rather than Iron Age, and although it may have been a place of refuge, it has been suggested that it served some unknown ceremonial purpose.

IRON AGE MASSACRE

Fin Cop is 8 miles south-east of Mam Tor, near Ashford-in-the-Water. As with many other places in the Peak District, the location had been inhabited for thousands of years by the time of the Iron Age. In addition to pottery chards dating from the Bronze Age, there is also evidence of chert knapping. In the Iron Age the story took a darker turn, with evidence of defences erected in haste, burning and of a mass grave. The first skeleton to be uncovered from beneath a fallen wall was that of a pregnant woman whose body had been thrown into the fort's ditch. Later excavations revealed more partial skeletons of women, all of childbearing age, and children, as well as the huddled remains of a teenage boy. There is no existing evidence of what happened to the men or older women from within the community, but there are still more than 390m of ditch to excavate. This hill fort has every indication of being attacked and its ramparts deliberately destroyed.

ROMANO-BRITISH DERBYSHIRE (C. AD 43–350)

By the beginning of the first century AD several tribes, including the Corieltauvi to the south of Derbyshire, influenced by continental Europe, which had fallen under Roman control, began producing their own coins alongside bartering for goods and services. A discovery at Reynard's Kitchen Cave in Dovedale, outside the territory controlled by the tribe, yielded a hoard of twenty-six coins dating from the late Iron Age, but the inclusion of three Roman coins and a brooch shows that it was buried after the invasion of Britain.

In AD 43, Emperor Claudius invaded Britain. Within four years, the Romans had control over parts of the south of the country. They called their new province Britannia.

QUEEN CARTIMANDUA AND THE ROMANS

Following Emperor Claudius's successful invasion, Queen Cartimandua of the Brigantes, who gained power over her tribe, allied herself with Rome. As a client kingdom, the Brigantes benefitted from trade with the Romans, who occupied the south of England, while fulfilling the role of a buffer zone between the Roman settlements in the south and hostile northern tribes. She was expected to pay taxes in the form of goods including slaves, hunting dogs and hawks, but the relationship ensured her position within her territory. The agreement, which meant that the Romans did not dominate Derbyshire, held for twenty years.

According to the Roman author Tacitus, the queen captured Caractacus, son of King Cunobelin who had ruled the defeated Catuvellauni and Trinovantes tribes, when he fled into her kingdom seeking a safe refuge from the victorious Romans. Cartimandua handed her prize to the Emperor Claudius, who paraded his captive through the streets of Rome to represent the defeat of the Britons. There was considerable resentment against the queen's pro-Roman policy, which resulted in rebellion in AD 48.

The Romans were forced to send the legion of the IX *Hispana* to support the queen. Soon after AD 50, by which time Nero was emperor, the Romans, who had been in Britain for less than a decade, crossed the Trent and built a new fort that they named *Derventio*, or Little Chester, a little to the north of modern Derby at Strutts Park. It was sited on high ground to protect the river crossing, the lowest point that could be forded, on the western side of the Derwent. Confident that potential trouble had been dealt with, the fort was soon abandoned. The garrison who manned it were needed elsewhere.

Cartimandua's husband, Venutius, rebelled against her in AD 69 when she divorced him and replaced him with his own armour bearer, Vellocatus. The queen needed rescuing once again but this time the Romans had problems of their own. That year saw four emperors rule in quick succession to one another and Rome fought its first civil war. In Britannia some of the legions rebelled, and its governor, Marcus Vettius Bolanus, was only able to send non-citizen auxiliaries to her aid rather than a legion of Romans. Tacitus records that the queen was evacuated to safety but the insurrection against her rule was not suppressed. History does not record Cartimandua's eventual fate.

DERBYSHIRE BECOMES PART OF BRITANNIA

In AD 73, acting on the orders of Emperor Vespasian, another governor of Britannia, Petillius Cerialis, waged a successful war against the Brigantes tribe and conquered the north of England including Derbyshire. The region's new rulers began to establish centres to manage the population and its resources.

In about AD 80, orders were given for a larger fort to be built at the modern Chester Green area of Derby. The eighteenth-century antiquarian William Stukeley visited Derby in 1724 and mapped the remains of the fort that were still visible, recording a stone wall and ditch as well as the fort's north and south gateways. Although nothing is evident today apart from some stone bases to columns at Marcus Street in Derby, the fort was the most important of Derbyshire's Roman garrisons, defending the river crossing and the region's military road network, which to start with were little more than tracks for moving men and equipment as quickly as possible. Archaeologists believe that the east bank of the River Derwent was lined with wharves and there may even have been a wooden bridge.

Only commanding officers were allowed to marry and for their families to accompany them, but it did not prevent ordinary soldiers from forming relationships with local women. A civilian settlement outside the fort at Derby, known as a *vicus,* accommodated these unofficial families alongside local inhabitants from the end of the second century onwards. As well as dwellings and a bath house, there is substantial evidence for metal working and pottery manufacture. Even in its early years Derby thrived as an industrial centre.

The growing population needed to be fed. At Ockbrook, to the east of Derby, the remains of a huge 29m-long and 12m-wide barn has been excavated. Evidence of Romano-British field systems are scattered across the county from Swarkestone to Glossop. No evidence of any well-appointed villas has been found in Derbyshire, unlike those excavated in the south of England. Instead, foundations show that a mixture of round British houses and rectangular Roman farmsteads, like the ones at Ockbrook or Roystone Grange at Ballidon, were preferred.

GUARDING THE PENNINES

During the AD 70s, military commander Agricola, in preparation for his advance deeper into Brigantes territory to the north, and into Scotland, ordered that a chain of forts and signal stations should be built on an east–west axis at *Navio* (Brough) above a bend in the River Noe; *Aquae Arnemetiae* (Buxton); and *Melandra* (Glossop). *Melandra* is 10 miles from a larger fort, *Mamucium*, at Castlefield in Manchester further west. The role of the line of Derbyshire forts, manned by cohorts of 500 men drawn from the provinces rather than Rome itself, was to guard the western side of the Pennines as well as the road network upon which the legions relied.

Among the finds at *Melandra* during excavations in the fort ditch was a leather sling, made from cow hide, the only one of its kind in Britain. Roman soldiers were trained to use a sling to hit a target 180m away, well out of range of enemy spears. A centurial stone, discovered at a nearby farm, built into the fort at the time of its construction to mark the work of the men responsible for building it, records the presence of the First Cohort of *Frisiavones*, an infantry auxiliary unit from Germany, and their commander Valerius Vitalis. Auxiliary cohorts were commanded by experienced professional soldiers who were not part of the tribe that formed the cohort.

Derbyshire's forts were originally built as earthworks with timber defences but were later rebuilt in stone. A centurial stone from *Navio* records its rebuilding in AD 154 by the First Cohort of the *Aquitanians* under the command of

Julius Verus. An altar dating from the same period was dedicated to the local water goddess *Arnemetia*. The regiment originally arrived in Britain to help build Hadrian's Wall but then remained. It is thought that *Navio* was abandoned after it fulfilled Agricola's purposes but then rebuilt in stone and re-garrisoned as the result of a local revolt against Roman rule. The *Cohors Prima Aquitanorum* were sent to Derbyshire as a visible reminder of Rome's power, and to ensure that the local inhabitants were bent to the will of the empire of which they were now a part. *Navio* was of strategic importance because it controlled the entrance to the Hope Valley and to Edale and its lead mines. The legionaries, from the south-west of France, may have dreamed of hotter summers and warmer winters while they were stationed in Derbyshire, but they signed on for twenty-five years. If they survived their service they became citizens, entitled to marry and also raise their children as citizens of Rome.

A fort in the north-east of the county at Chesterfield or *Caesterfeld* was constructed early in the Roman occupation of the region, but in about AD 80–100 the original fort was demolished, and another, smaller one built close to the first, though it was only occupied for about forty years before being abandoned. It was perhaps the third fortification to be built on the hill there. *Caester* may refer to the Roman fort, but it might also mean an old fortification or earthwork. When the legions arrived, they sited their fort in the same place as an Iron Age earthwork. An archaeological survey has revealed the remains of an Iron Age ditch was backfilled during the fort's construction.

Although the soldiers left during the second century AD, Roman *Caesterfeld* flourished for a brief time. There is evidence of industrial ovens and furnaces associated with iron working, dating from AD 130. The location was convenient for the nearby Ryknield Street and raw resources for metal working were readily available. No evidence for occupation, military or civil, has been found after the second century.

Derbyshire's first tourist destination

Buxton, identified on the *Ravenna Cosmography*'s list of all the known places in the world in about AD 700, became an important regional centre dedicated to the Celtic goddess *Arnemetia*. The Romans often adopted local gods by finding parallels between them and their own gods.

Buxton is likely to have had a fort, although it has never been discovered and excavated, and a spa as well as being the hub of a road network. The thermal springs produced water at a temperature of 28° Celsius. The Romans built a bath, making Buxton one of only two bath towns in Britain; the other being Bath in Gloucestershire, or *Aquae Sulis* as the Romans knew it. They created a 20m-long and 7m-wide bath, as well as a 2m-square lead cistern, both of which were excavated in 1695 by Cornelius White, who ran the baths at the end of the seventeenth century. Other cisterns, part of a huge cast-iron cauldron and some of the structures of the baths were discovered during the eighteenth century when the 5th Duke of Devonshire developed Buxton as a fashionable spa.

There is much evidence of Roman activity in Buxton. Fragments of Samian pottery, glass, buildings, roof tiles, a temple and altars and an inscribed milestone have been found. In 1917, a hoard of coins was uncovered at the baths in Buxton. They cover 300 years of Roman emperors from the beginning to the end of imperial occupation of Britannia. Visitors to the sacred waters gave the coins as offerings to the water gods, just as today pennies are still thrown into wells and fountains for good luck.

Bronzesmiths in Buxton

Romano-British smiths at Poole's Cavern, a site occupied since 2000 BC, near Buxton, created popular items of jewellery including a bronze and enamel brooch, dolphin and trumpet-style brooches made from copper, or copper alloys, as well as bangles, pendants, rings and earrings. The families who made the jewellery lived and worked in, or near, the caves. Among the finds were coins, fragments of pottery, animal bones and human burials.

As well as the finished product, excavations found fragments of unworked metal bars; a small crucible; solidified metal droplets from the smelting process; and the excess metal left from pouring molten metal into a mould known as casting sprue. Further evidence of jewellery production including brooches, a bronze armband, and a set composed of bronze tweezers, ear scoop and nail cleaner has also been found at Thirst House Cave in Deepdale near Buxton. In all likelihood the decorative metal work was being produced by British smiths to supply wealthy Roman visitors to the town, as well as soldiers on leave, with souvenirs of their visit to *Aquae Arnemetiae*.

LEAD MINING AND THE LOST TOWN OF *LUTUDARUM*

The Romans were quick to exploit Derbyshire's lead deposits. They put it to diverse uses, from pipes, roofing and tableware to coffins and weights. Pliny the Elder wrote that lead veins were so abundant that its production was strictly limited to control the market price. Mines, such as the Odin Mine near Castleton, were worked by convicted criminals whose lives could be measured in months once they arrived in Derbyshire.

After the ore was mined, the convicts smelted it. This was done by digging a hole, or a bole, on the top of a hill, with its mouth facing into prevailing wind. Wood and lead ore were placed in the boles, where they were set alight. Molten lead was channelled into moulds that solidified into bars of lead called 'pigs'. Bolehill near Wirksworth is an example of where the Romans cited their lead hearths near to the site of their mines. Most lead ore was smelted this way until the sixteenth century.

Archaeological evidence of Roman lead mining is provided by the discovery of pigs of lead bearing inscriptions, LVT, LVTVD or LVTDARES. The abbreviations stand for *Lutudarum*, which was the administrative centre of the Roman mining operation in Derbyshire according to the *Ravenna Cosmography*. Its exact geographic location remains something of a mystery. Carsington, Wirksworth and Crich have all been suggested. An extensive Romano-British settlement was identified at Carsington, complete with a cupellation plant where the Romans are likely to have tried to separate silver from the lead. Unfortunately, the area is now beneath Carsington Reservoir. None of the evidence is conclusive and the location of *Lutudarum* remains subject to conjecture.

DERBYSHIRE WARE

The Romans built three kilns at Hazelwood near Derby during the third century AD. The area was abundant in wood, water and gritty grey clay, which potters threw to create storage jars in various sizes, with a rim inside the neck upon which a lid might rest. Another cluster of kilns was located at Holbrook, almost 6 miles further east. Both sites made and fired Derbyshire Ware pottery, which emerged in a variety of colours, from grey to purple, for 150 years from AD 140 onwards. The pots have been found at army sites across the north of Britain and in Wales as well as more locally.

ROMAN ROADS IN DERBYSHIRE

The pattern of land use continued as it had during the Iron Age, with farming in the Trent Valley and in the upland areas of the county. People moved around using trackways that had existed since Prehistoric times. The Romans built their own roads for military movement but engineered some of the existing network to provide better communication:

- Ryknield, or Icknield, Street was an important military artery that cut a path south-west where it connected to Lichfield and then to Fosse Way in Gloucestershire. To the north it linked Derby to Chesterfield before joining to the Roman fort at Templeborough in South Yorkshire.
- A road ran south-east from the fort at Derby to the River Trent at Sawley, ensuring a connection with water traffic. A section of the road was uncovered in 1910 near Derby's racecourse. At the time it was described as being 12ft wide and metalled.
- 'The Street' ran from Derby to Buxton through the Derbyshire Dales and High Peak in a north-west direction. Its midpoint was the lead-producing settlement at Lutudarum, which was centred somewhere between Wirksworth and Carsington. Parts of the road were provided with a raised embankment and a straight alignment that can be seen today in a 14-mile stretch of field boundaries near Minning Low, where traces of the road are lost.
- 'Batham Gate' ran south-west from Templeborough to the spa town of Buxton, continuing to the Roman fort near Brough. It is thought that this road crosses Stanage Edge where it makes a steep descent. It is paved with large rutted slabs of gritstone. However, it is impossible to date and it has recently been suggested the track that is marked as Roman on maps is more probably medieval.
- To the west a road, later known as 'Doctor Gate', led across the moors from Glossop to Brough.
- 'Hereward Street' started at the Roman fort at Rocester, heading north-east through Ellastone and Mayfield near Ashbourne, forded the River Derwent at Cromford, before continuing to the fort at Chesterfield.

There are other sections of road recorded in the Peak District and further south, including the prehistoric Portway that ran north-west across Derbyshire from Stapleford in Nottinghamshire via Wirksworth to Mam Tor. Roman roads served the purpose of linking forts and industrial centres into an efficient network. Some of the routes, long established before the legions arrived, continued to be used after they left. For example, the Roman road from Buxton to the fort of *Condate* in Northwich, Cheshire, became the route of the 1759 turnpike road running from Buxton to Macclesfield, while the A5020 from Derby to Burton follows Ryknield Street.

The Amber Valley Hoard and the end of Rome

In about AD 260, Britannia, together with Gaul and Spain, broke away from the rest of the Roman Empire forming an independent territory, which was reabsorbed into the Roman Empire in AD 274. As a result of the conflict, Britain – including the people of Derbyshire – experienced economic difficulties.

The Amber Valley Hoard, discovered by a metal detectorist in 2010 near Ripley, contained 3,631 coins called radiates hidden beneath the remains of a Roman house thought to date from the third or fourth century. All but four of the radiates were counterfeit. The Romano-British population of Derbyshire, who were used to a coin-based economy, dealt with a lack of coinage caused by civil unrest by making their own rudimentary copies of the currency in bronze.

It was not the only coin hoard to be discovered in Derbyshire. In 1890, during work on the Great Northern Branch Railway, an earthenware jar containing more than 1,000 coins was found at Shipley, but they were distributed among the crowd gathered there. More than a century earlier, at the end of November 1748, the discovery of gold coins in Alfreton at Codnor Park during the creation of a drain sparked a treasure-hunting frenzy. For ten days people flocked to the area. The Society of Antiquaries reported that 3,000 coins were eventually recovered.

Coin offerings at Buxton came to an abrupt halt and occupation of the fort at *Derventio* came to an end in the fourth century. By about AD 350 the Roman cemetery flanking the road going east from Derby, as well as an enclosed cemetery beyond the industrial quarter, were no longer in use. The Romano-British population of Derbyshire were left to manage their own affairs.

SAXON DERBYSHIRE

During the fifth century, the Romano-British population of Derbyshire settled down to life outside the empire. Over time supply chains that had once kept the legions fed failed. The population reverted to barter, and trade became more local. Without the need to transport perishable goods across an empire, the pottery kilns outside Derby fell into disrepair.

Parts of north Derbyshire came under the influence of the kingdom of Elmet, which extended south from modern Cumbria, but evidence is scarce. It is certain that Britain divided into regional kingdoms that probably reflected the tribal boundaries of earlier times. The whole country was open for settlement by the Germanic peoples. By the middle of the sixth century, Saxons began to migrate inland along the Trent and Derwent valleys. One of the first areas they settled was at Repton in South Derbyshire, which became the capital of the kingdom of Mercia.

Many place names in Derbyshire derive from Saxon habitation. Ashbourne originates from the Old English meaning a stream with ash trees. Places ending in *-lea* can mean that there was once a woodland or a clearing in a woodland. A *tun* element in a name shows that there was a farmstead or a village, while locations ending in *-worth* mean that there was an Anglo-Saxon enclosure nearby. And, of course, the

Saxons wanted to stamp their ownership on the land that they claimed for themselves. For instance, Bonsall near Matlock belonged to a Saxon called Brunt.

The upland areas of the Peak District were the last parts of Derbyshire to be occupied by the new tribes, which is why the region still retains a significant number of place names reflective of its Romano-British past. For example, Crich derives from the Celtic name for hill, while anywhere with the element *eccles* comes from the Roman word for a church. The River Dove has nothing to do with birds, it results from the Old British word meaning 'black or dark'. The first half of Kinder Scout's name is even thought to pre-date the region's Iron Age inhabitants.

THE GREY DITCH

The Grey Ditch, crossing the dale at Bradwell in the Hope Valley, is an earthwork created from a bank and a deep ditch, which runs across the north of the Peak District from Mam Tor to Shatton Edge near Hope. It is thought to have marked a barrier between kingdoms, or even to have shown the boundary of the territory belonging to the Romano-British population who maintained control of the gritstone uplands even after the Saxons claimed the rest of the region. There is even a possible reference to the ditch in the *Anglo-Saxon Chronicle* for AD 942. It identifies a boundary separating the kingdoms of Deira and Mercia, approximating to modern-day Yorkshire and Derbyshire, which could have incorporated the Grey Ditch.

KING EDWIN AND THE BATTLE OF WIN HILL

Local legend states that a battle was fought near to Castleton, also in the Hope Valley, in AD 626 when Edwin, King of Deira, fought against Cwichelm of Wessex and Penda of Mercia. According to the story, an army led by Edwin chose a strong point at Win Hill, where they created a defence from a temporary wall of stones. The forces of Wessex and Mercia grouped on Lose Hill, which lies on the other side of the River Noe. When the armies of Cwichelm and Penda charged up towards Edwin's men, they were crushed by rocks that the Deirans hurled down upon them.

A second legend associated with Edwin's territorial campaign to claim land in Derbyshire for himself maintains that, after an unspecified battle, the king was captured and hanged from the Edwin or Eden Tree north of the village of Bradwell. Sadly, without evidence there is no historical basis for either tale, but the stories persist. The Grey Ditch may have been an indication of Mercian possession and dominance in the Hope Valley. The area's mineral wealth and the existence of two Roman roads passing through, or close by, Bradwell account for the lingering memories of conflict in the area during the Early Medieval period.

THE PEAK DISTRICT GETS ITS NAME

It is likely, across much of Derbyshire, that people continued to live and die much as they had been doing since before the legions withdrew. The people of the Peak, or the *Pecsaetan* from which the name Peak District derives, were recorded by Mercian tax collectors in the late seventh century, when the 'Tribal Hidage', land that each group of people possessed was drawn up to assess the kingdom's taxable value for tribute to be paid to the king.

THE BENTY GRANGE HELMET

Thirty-eight burial mounds in the Peak District are known to contain interments from the Anglo-Saxon period. Grave goods found with many of the burials suggest that the people were pagans rather than Christians, but there was a gradual change in belief systems.

A seventh-century barrow burial at Benty Grange near Monyash, excavated in 1848 by Thomas Bateman, revealed the remains of a helmet. It was the first Anglo-Saxon helmet to be discovered in England. It was made from an iron frame covered with riveted horn plates. Its crest was decorated with a boar, associated with the goddess Freya, reflecting its owner's pagan past, while the metal cross on the nose guard identified the warrior's newfound beliefs, or at least his hope that the Christian symbol might offer some protection in battle.

CHRISTIANITY ARRIVES IN DERBYSHIRE

There is no evidence to confirm what people in Derbyshire believed when Emperor Constantine first legalised Christianity in about AD 200, or whether Christianity continued to be practised by its Romano-British population after the legions withdrew.

Christianity gradually spread through the Anglo-Saxon kingdoms. Peada, a son of Penda, King of Mercia, described by the Venerable Bede as 'an excellent youth', converted to Christianity along with his nobility when he married a Northumbrian princess at Repton in AD 653. The Northumbrians sent four priests to ensure that the Mercians fulfilled the conditions under which the marriage took place. In AD 656, Diuma, one of the four, became the first Bishop of Mercia.

St Betti, another of the priests, is said to have founded the church at Wirksworth that became the base for his missionary work in Derbyshire. The richly sculpted lid of his coffin, known as the Wirksworth Stone, can be found in the parish church of St Mary. Carvings depict scenes from the life of Christ, shown as the Lamb of God. These were preserved by the current church's medieval builders. The stone was rediscovered upside-down beneath the chancel floor, close to the altar, in 1820.

At Derby, known by the Saxons as Northworthy, a new church acted as a centre from which priests could be sent to other areas. Carved crosses began to dot the upland areas of Derbyshire as more of the Peak District's inhabitants became Christian. They date from AD 600–1000, and can still be found in many places throughout Derbyshire. Historians dispute whether they are Northumbrian, Mercian or even Scandinavian in origin. Crosses can also be found in the churchyards at Bakewell, Bradbourne, Hope and Eyam, which has been described as Derbyshire's finest example of an Anglian cross, with decorations that include angels blowing trumpets. The cross shaft at Bakewell is 2.4m tall. There is also a collection of early medieval cross fragments mingled with carved tomb pieces in the church porch discovered during its rebuilding in the nineteenth century.

MERCIAN KINGS OF DERBYSHIRE

By AD 653, Paeda had established a double abbey at Repton where both monks and nuns lived. He also built a palace for himself there. The abbey became the burial place for three Mercian kings, including King Æthelbald, who was murdered at the hands of his own bodyguards in AD 757. It is likely that the surviving Anglo-Saxon crypt beneath Repton's church, which he built, was also Æthelbald's mausoleum.

The Repton Stone, part of a cross shaft, shows an armed man on horseback with a sword and shield raised in the air. He also appears to be wearing a crown. It is possible that the carving depicts Æthelbald, who was one of Mercia's most powerful kings.

In AD 849, Wigstan, another member of the royal family, was murdered by his guardian and buried at Repton. Soon rumours of miracles at Wigstan's tomb spread and Repton became a place of pilgrimage. Wigstan, later known as Wystan, was canonised, and is the patron saint of the current parish church that was built in the thirteenth and fourteenth centuries. His remains were removed from the abbey during the rule of King Cnut in the eleventh century to Evesham Abbey in Worcestershire, which had its own associations with the Mercian royal family.

T'OWD MAN OF WIRKSWORTH

During the eighth century, Repton Abbey gained control of lead mining at Wirksworth. A small carved figure of a miner with a pick and workman's basket, or kibble, dating from the Saxon period is carved on one of the stones in the south transept of St Mary's Church, Wirksworth. The old man, or 'T'Owd Man' as the carving is known, was found during the restoration of the largely fourteenth-century St James' Church in the nearby village of Bonsall. T'Owd Man is thought to have originated from an earlier church on the same site and was reused as part of the foundations of the medieval building. From there he found his way to the garden of the local churchwarden, John Broxup Coates. At some time between 1870 and 1874, T'Owd Man was rescued from his role as a garden ornament and incorporated into the walls of St Mary's, which was undergoing its own restoration. The carving is thought to be Britain's earliest representation of a miner.

DERBYSHIRE'S HERMIT KING

In about AD 806, Eardwulf, the King of Northumbria, was deposed during a struggle for the Northumbrian throne. He sought refuge in the kingdom of Mercia near Repton where, it is believed, he lived as a hermit in the Anchor Church Caves between Foremark and Ingleby.

The caves, cut out of a sandstone cliff, were originally thought to been created during the eighteenth century as a folly, but more recent research suggests that the dwelling is Saxon in origin. A sixteenth-century text, as well as local folklore, links the cave to Hardulph, another name for Eardwulf. The deposed king eventually travelled to Rome, where he visited Pope Leo II, and to the court of Charlemagne, the king of the Franks, at Nijmegen, before returning to Mercia and then to his own kingdom accompanied by envoys from the pope. It is unclear whether he resumed his throne or was driven back into exile.

DERBY GETS A PATRON SAINT

In AD 819, Alkmund of Northumbria was, according to legend, killed by marauding Danes. Another, more likely, account states that the unfortunate prince, known for his care of the poor, was assassinated nineteen years earlier by King Eardwulf to prevent him from ever becoming king. His father and brother had already been murdered during a brutal dynastic struggle over the crown of Northumbria. Whatever the truth, Alkmund was quickly recognised as a martyr and then a saint.

He was buried first at Lilleshall in Shropshire but then, because of Viking raids, his body was moved to Derby. The coffin bearers moving Alkmund's remains paused to rest near Duffield. Healing waters were said to have sprung from the ground where the coffin rested. St Alkmund's Well, as it came to be known, was credited for its healing powers throughout the Middle Ages. The cortege continued into Derby, and the body of Alkmund was laid to rest. Soon afterwards miracles were reported. His cult became popular in the Midlands as pilgrims made the journey to Derby in hope of a cure. The church where he was buried, on the northern outskirts of the town, was rededicated to him and he became Derby's patron saint.

It was not the end of Alkmund's travels though. He was relocated back to Shropshire during the tenth century at a time when Derby was on the front line of a series of battles between the Saxons and the Vikings. It was only in 1145, when England was in the grip of the civil war between Empress Matilda and King Stephen, that the saint's body made the journey back to Derby.

In 1968, the Victorian church of St Alkmund's, which stood on the site of the original ninth-century church where Alkmund was buried, was demolished to make way for

Derby's inner ring road. Excavations uncovered the remains of previous medieval churches as well as the original building. An ornate stone sarcophagus and fragments of a 4m-tall stone cross were discovered during the work.

It was originally thought that the coffin was part of St Alkmund's shrine, but more recently it has been argued that it is the tomb of Ealdorman Æthelwulf, who was described by the *Anglo-Saxon Chronicle* as being part of King Alfred's great army. He fought against the Vikings at Ashdown, in Berkshire, where he was killed in AD 871. Afterwards, Æthelwulf's body was secretly carried to Derby, where it was buried.

THE GREAT HEATHEN ARMY: THE VIKINGS ARRIVE IN DERBYSHIRE

Many boatloads of Danes arrived on English shores in AD 865. Their leaders were Halfdan, Ubba and Ivar the Boneless. The Great Heathen Army, as the Saxons called it, spent much of the next thirteen years plundering. In AD 867, York, which was Northumbria's capital, fell to the army before it overwintered in Nottingham. In the spring of AD 868, men from Derbyshire found themselves in the Saxon militia, or fyrd as it was known, attempting to dislodge the invaders, who now turned their attention on Mercia. King Burgred of Mercia put aside his differences with King Æthelred of Wessex so that armies from both kingdoms could lay siege to the Danes in their camp at Nottingham. The Saxons were unable to defeat them. Burgred eventually paid tribute, called Danegeld, to the Vikings in return for them returning to Northumbria.

In the winter of AD 873, the army, several thousand strong by that time, sailed up the River Trent and captured the Mercian capital at Repton. By then Burgred had come to terms with the Vikings on three separate occasions, but now his kingdom was overrun and he was driven into exile.

That winter, AD 873–74, part of the Viking army over-wintered at Repton amid the ruins of the devastated abbey, foraged for supplies and tended to their sick. Archaeological finds at Foremark, a few miles further down river, suggest that the rest of the army camped nearby. Repton's abbey church was used as a gatehouse permitting entrance to the Viking camp. They dug a D-shaped ditch and rampart around the abbey, with its straight edge to the river allowing vessels to moor safely. There was even a slipway so that the Vikings could draw their longboats onto the shore.

A KING'S TOMB

A huge communal grave outside Repton's defensive rampart was found to contain 264 people, of whom 80 per cent were men of fighting age. The majority of bodies lacked hand and feet bones, leading to the conclusion that most of the bodies were exhumed from their original resting places and relocated to the tomb at Repton. However, the lack of obvious injury to the bones complicates the idea that they were the remains of men who died in battle. Illness is a more likely cause of death in the circumstances. The skeletons were disarticulated, sorted and stacked around a central cist that, according to an eighteenth-century report of the cairn's first excavation, contained the skeleton of a very tall person, since lost. The body in the cist must have been a high-status leader to have been afforded the burial he was given.

It may have been Ivar the Boneless who was buried at Repton. According to the saga of Ragnar Hairy-breeks, Ivar was born with weak bones as the result of a curse. He allegedly came to England with his brothers and their men to exact vengeance for the death of his father, Ragnor, who was thrown into a pit of snakes by Ælla, King of Northumbria. When Ivar and his brothers caught up with Ælla at York in AD 867, they executed him using the blood eagle. The ritual method of execution involved cracking the ribcage open from behind and pulling the victim's lungs out from inside their body to make a wing-like shape.

Afterwards the Viking army advanced on Mercia and Wessex. Ivar was identified as one of its commanders, but it is probable that he died during the winter of AD 869–70 as he is not mentioned again by the *Anglo-Saxon Chronicle*. If this was the case, he was also moved from his original place of burial prior to being placed in the cist at Repton. Irish chronicles of the period identify Ivar as a king of Dublin, and describe his death between the years AD 870 and 873. *The Fragmentary Annals of Ireland* are alone in stating that Ivar's death was caused by a sudden and horrible disease, which could refer to the condition with which he was born or the epidemic that appears to have killed many of the Great Heathen Army.

The mound at Repton is not isolated. There are other graves clustered around the area. One man, buried with five silver pennies, was laid to rest in the rubble and burned timbers of the church. Another of the graves, Grave 511, contained a double burial. One of the skeletons was of a man likely to have been killed by the spear wounds inflicted to his head above his eye and a violent blow with an axe or a sword to his hip and pelvis as he lay injured on the ground. He was buried with his sword, a Thor's hammer amulet and a boar's tusk placed as a symbolic penis instead of the one he lost when he was wounded.

Heath Wood at Ingleby, close to Repton, is home to England's only known Viking cremation cemetery, with fifty-nine cremation mounds containing splinters of bone and metal fragments, as well as the remnants of animals that may have been offerings or essential companions in the afterlife, including horses and dogs. It was first surveyed by Thomas Bateman, the Barrow Knight, in 1855, who opened five of them. More recent excavations reveal that the mounds were made by constructing a ring ditch with an embankment of earth in the centre. A pyre and wooden platform were placed on top of the mound. The body was burned, accompanied by weapons and other belongings. Today the cemetery is lost in woodland, but in the ninth century the pyres sat on heathland overlooking the Trent Valley.

VIKING SETTLEMENT IN DERBYSHIRE

Before the Heathen Army renewed its campaign against the Saxons in the spring of AD 874, the Vikings installed Ceolwulf as their client king of Mercia. When they next returned to the Midlands, they began to settle in Derbyshire.

They refortified the Roman walls at *Derventio*. In time they rebuilt the town but called it *Deorby*, or 'the town of the deer'. Derbyshire became a border zone at the edge of Viking rule. A lack of Scandinavian place names in the west and north of the county show that there was not wholesale settlement, although the Vikings were quick to establish control over the lead fields around Wirksworth. Kirk Ireton was once the home of a Viking who originated from Ireland. Place names ending in *-holme* along the Dove Valley show that the Vikings made their homes on raised dry ground thereabouts. Thorpe, near Ashbourne, was an outlying farm that belonged to a Scandinavian settler. Many other place names, including Ashford, show that the new settlers adapted existing place names into their own language, although that did not mean that the two groups lived together. Rowsley near Matlock was named by the Saxons as a woodland clearing, but the first part of the modern place name indicated that it was claimed by a Viking called *Hrólfr*. Denby, to the south-east of the county, translates as 'a village of the Danes'.

THE VIKINGS BECOME CHRISTIAN

In AD 878, King Alfred of Wessex defeated the Scandinavians at the Battle of Edington, Wiltshire. He negotiated the Treaty of Wedmore with Guthrum, their leader, in AD 880, dividing England between them and creating a part of the country known as Danelaw. Alfred retained Wessex and part of Mercia, including London. The Vikings would have East Anglia and everything north of Watling Street, including Derbyshire.

Under the terms of Guthrum's agreement with King Alfred, the Viking leader was baptised into the Christian faith. In time Scandinavians living in Derbyshire set aside their pagan beliefs. There are two notable cross shafts near Ashbourne reflecting the changing beliefs of the Vikings. One, in the churchyard at Brailsford, illustrates a Viking warrior with shield and sword. It is thought to date from the tenth century by its style. A fragment of a second cross shaft depicting a Viking is located in Norbury Church. Both crosses may have been created in memory of specific individuals.

VIKING GOVERNMENT AND ADMINISTRATION

Derby became one of the five burghs, or main towns, of Danish-controlled Mercia. It was ruled by a *jarl,* or earl, who managed his lands from its base. They divided the region into administrative areas called *wapentakes*. The word means 'the taking of weapons'. Chief men gathering at official meetings clashed their swords together to express their agreement. The meetings were usually held at a crossroads, near a river, or at significant markers in the landscape such as standing stones, trees or mounds.

Derbyshire's wapentakes, by the eleventh century, were Scarsdale, Hamestan, Morlestan or Morleyton, Walecross and Appletree. The meeting place for Morlestan was at Morley, although the location of the stone where the meetings were held is unknown. The original gathering place at Appletree is also unknown, but by the fourteenth century the local court was held at Sutton on the Hill. A later Norman survey also identified a district called *Peche-fers* or the Peak Forest.

LADY OF THE MERCIANS

Æthelflaed, the daughter of King Alfred the Great of Wessex, known as the Lady of the Mercians, married Ethelred, King of Mercia, in AD 886 when she was 14 years old. The union sealed an alliance between the two kingdoms. Æthelflaed soon won a reputation for both her intelligence and fighting skills, which even impressed the Vikings. War raged in and around the south of Derbyshire as she battled to regain the northern part of her husband's kingdom.

In AD 902, Æthelflaed became the joint ruler of Mercia. After Ethelred's death in AD 911, she ruled in her own right, leading an army against the Vikings and regaining most of the territory that they had annexed from Mercia in the Midlands. In July of AD 917, the queen advanced from Nottingham to Derby. According to the *Anglo-Saxon Chronicle*, a fierce battle took place, 'and with the help of God she obtained the borough which is called Derby with all that belongs to it'.

KING EDWARD THE ELDER AND
THE SAXON KINGS OF 'ALL ENGLAND'

In AD 919, shortly after the Lady of Mercia's death, Æthelflaed's brother, King Edward of Wessex, deposed Æthelflaed's daughter, Aelfwynn, from her throne and claimed Mercia for himself. Saxons and Scandinavians submitted to his rule.

The following year he issued orders for a new burgh to be built at Derby, and for another to be built on his realm's north-eastern border at Bakewell, where the River Wye might be easily forded. All Saints' Church, parts of which have been dated to AD 920, was built at the same time. The settlement was of importance to the secular and religious administration of the Peak District. It was also a strategic base for Edward. When his fort was completed at Bakewell, the king invited Northern leaders to meet with him there. The *Anglo-Saxon Chronicle* recorded that all the people who lived in Northumbria and Strathclyde recognised his overlordship. If the chronicle is taken at face value, the Treaty of Bakewell ensured that Edward of Wessex became England's overlord. In reality, the agreement was more likely to have created a pact between the kings against the Viking rulers of York and Ireland.

Not everyone in Mercia was happy with the arrangement that placed the kings of Wessex on the Mercian throne. In AD 924, shortly before his death, some of Edward's reluctant subjects revolted against him. It was a time of uncertainty

for the people of Derby, as first one side and then the other seized the town. The Danes briefly recaptured Derby before it was taken by King Athelstan of Wessex in AD 937, who established a royal mint there. Two years later, the death of Athelstan left a power vacuum that prompted the Danes to reconquer the Five Burghs, or Boroughs of the Midlands, including Derby. In AD 942, King Edmund I of Wessex, the king of 'all England' according to the *Anglo-Saxon Chronicle*, seized Derby once more.

DERBY AND ALL SAINTS CHURCH

The new burgh built at Derby in the 920s on King Edward the Elder's orders was on land that belonged to the Crown. It lay between the River Derwent to the east and the Markeaton Brook to the west. A deep ditch was created to the north of the new site of the town. The land inside the burgh was divided into long strips called burgage plots, with a narrow frontage aligned to the north–south road. It was a sufficiently important place to have its own mint. Coins struck stated the place of their origin – *Deorabi*. These continued to be minted, providing coin for Derbyshire until the Norman Conquest in 1066.

King Edward also gave orders for a new minster to be built, dedicated to all the saints. It was served by a sub-dean and six canons, one more than at St Alkmund's, which lay to the north of the new town. It meant that All Saints was the most important church in the burgh. The king granted his church land to support itself at Little Chester. In addition, each of the seven canons were assigned income from nearby farms at Quarndon and Little Eaton. Even more important, All Saints was designated a royal free chapel. This meant that it was not subject to the authority of a bishop, who could not appoint clerics to it. And, it was free from the obligation of paying taxes to the diocese in which it stood.

THE RISE AND FALL OF MORCAR OF MERCIA

Wulfric Spot was a very wealthy man even though he was only a *thegn*, which meant he was a noble with less power than an earl. His family gained estates across the Midlands through service to King Edmund I of Wessex and to his brother, Edgar, who became king in AD 959. Spot was both powerful and influential. It is not clear exactly when he died, but King Æthelred the Unready issued a charter in 1004 confirming the thegn's will.

Under the terms of the will, Spot, who had no surviving sons, left much of his property in Derbyshire to the abbey at Burton that he founded. Morcar, another of Mercia's thegns and possibly married to Wulfric's granddaughter or a niece, also benefited. Wulfric's brother and son, Æflhelm and Wulfheah, were the main beneficiaries of the will. They did not have long to enjoy their inheritance. In 1006, the Earl of Mercia, Eadric Streona, which translates as 'the grasping', arranged for the murder of Æflhelm and the blinding of both his sons with the connivance of the king.

Morcar was fortunate in retaining King Æthelred's favour. He was described as the king's 'minister' or thegn, and received royal grants that included land in Derbyshire during the years 1009 to 1012. His possessions included estates in and around Smalley near Heanor; Morley in Erewash; land at Crich; Eckington to the north-east of the county; and Mickleover near Derby. Morcar wielded significant power in Mercia because of the strategic locations he held. He controlled the river crossings at Weston-on-Trent and at Great Wilne on the border with Leicestershire. Additionally, many of Morcar's estates lay alongside Ryknield Street, which meant that he had some control over access to the south from Yorkshire.

In 1013, King Sweyn Forkbeard of Denmark invaded England and forced Æthelred to flee. The Dane died the following February. The chief men of the Five Boroughs, including Morcar, immediately elected Sweyn's son, Cnut, to succeed his father. For Morcar and his brother it was an opportunity to become even more influential, but other nobles backed the return of Æthelred, and by April, Cnut was forced to leave England. Although he was unaware of it, Morcar's decision spelled the end of his good fortune.

The Saxon king punished the areas of Danelaw and its leaders for their support of Cnut. Early in 1015, a meeting was held in Oxford. Morcar and his brother travelled there believing that they were protected by Æthelred's promise of pardon. Instead, Eadric Streona murdered Morcar and his brother and the king seized both men's estates across the Midlands, including Morcar's lands in Derbyshire. The action emphasised the king's complicity in the deaths of the two men. The murders impacted on national politics as well as the balance of power in Derbyshire. Men who owed their loyalty to the dead thegns shifted their allegiance from the king to his eldest surviving son, Edmund Ironside, with whom Æthelred was in dispute.

THE EARLDOM OF MERCIA

King Æthelred became fatally ill and died on 23 April 1016. His son, Edmund Ironside, died that same year. That Christmas, Cnut was crowned king of England and married Æthelred's wife, Emma of Normandy. In future, he ordered, Saxons and Danes would live peaceably together. He divided England into four earldoms. Derbyshire was part of Mercia. Eadric Streona was appointed as its earl, but in 1017 Cnut discovered that Streona was complicit in the death of Edmund Ironside and had him executed.

DERBYSHIRE GETS ITS FIRST MENTION

The *Anglo-Saxon Chronicle* named Derbyshire for the first time in 1048. By then King Cnut was dead and King Æthelred the Unready's son, Edward the Confessor, was on the throne.

Throughout the period, Saxon and Danish kings acquired more of Derbyshire's land and mineral rights for themselves. Among the manors held by the Crown were Chesterfield and Newbold to the north-east of the county. The *Anglo-Saxon Chronicle* was less concerned by the distribution of resources than by the fact that on 1 May 1048 there was an earthquake that was felt in Derby, and which is believed to have caused destruction elsewhere in the county; a wildfire that did much damage in the countryside; and a plague that killed men and cattle across the country.

2

NORMAN DERBYSHIRE (1066–1154)

When Edward the Confessor died at the beginning of 1066, he was succeeded by his brother-in-law, Harold Godwinson. On 14 October, King Harold was killed, alongside most of his thegns, at Hastings by Duke William of Normandy. Although it was later claimed that Derby was emptied of able-bodied men who followed the king to defend his crown, the people of Derbyshire may have expected that little would change even if there was a new king. For the peasants, 70 per cent of the population, who worked land they rented when they were not obliged to work for their overlords, this was true. For the earls, thegns and even ceorls who owned their own land, the Norman Conquest would have lasting consequences.

Norman society was based on a feudal system. Rather than landowners having absolute rights over their property as they had in earlier times, King William controlled all the land in his domain. In return for their fealty, he gave estates to principal tenants who, in turn, gave some of their property to lesser nobility and knights who offered them their own loyalty and service. A single manor, or knight's fee, contained enough resources to provide for a knight, his family, and to equip him for all that he needed on the battlefield in order to fulfil his military obligations to his feudal overlord.

Even if families who owned property in Derbyshire before the conquest retained their manors and estates, they would not be able to do what they wished with them. They were expected to offer homage and service in return for their land holdings, either to the king himself or to one of the new men to whom he granted holdings. Instead of being landowners they became tenants or, even, sub-tenants. In 1069–70, men from the former kingdom of Mercia, including Derbyshire, rose under the leadership of Eadric the Wild against their new Norman overlords.

Resistance to the new order was put down with increasing savagery. King William adopted a policy of 'harrying' the north to deter further rebellion and to consolidate his regime. Circumstantial evidence points to Derbyshire suffering its share of reprisals. By the time of the Domesday Book, compiled in 1086, forty-three previously occupied settlements were described as waste, including, for example, the village of Hartington in the Peak District. At Eckington, to the north of the county, the value of the manor had dropped from £7 to 60s and the church was gone. Even some of the manors that William inherited from Edward the Confessor as royal estates, or *Terra Regis*, such as the ones at Ashbourne and Matlock Bridge, were described as partial waste. The majority of the Wapentake of Scarsdale, of which Chesterfield was a part and which belonged to the Crown, showed a reduction in value or was described as 'waste'.

NORMAN DERBY

Of the 352 locations listed by the Domesday Book in the county, Derby was by far the largest town with 140 households. Even so, it had shrunk by almost half since the conquest. There were 243 householders or burgesses before 1066. It was believed that the total population numbered about 1,100 before 1066, but this had reduced to approximately 630 in the years following the Norman invasion. The number of mills that ground wheat to provide flour for Derby's inhabitants dropped from fourteen to ten in the twenty years between the conquest and the Domesday survey.

Although the Normans built a motte and bailey castle at Cockpit Hill, first recorded in 1085, they did not erect a stone fortification on the same site, or elsewhere in Derby, at a later date. Instead, they consolidated their power at Nottingham, where the Sheriff of Nottingham's appointment covered Derbyshire and its Royal Forests. It was only in 1566 that separate choices were made for the two counties. It meant that the shire, or county, court was held at Nottingham rather than Derby and that the former became a centre of commerce with its own charter. It was a severe setback for Derby, which lost valuable trade as a consequence. In addition, a third of all revenue, known as the 'third penny', was payable to the king or his appointed representatives.

NORMAN GOVERNMENT AND ADMINISTRATION

The Normans adopted the Saxon system of dividing shires into hundreds, which roughly corresponded to the administrative role of the Scandinavian wapentake. Each hundred was originally either defined as an area capable of supporting a hundred families or a particular area of productive land. Every hundred held its own court to deal with property disputes, keeping the peace and feudal dues. The Normans and their successors used the administrative system to collect tax based on the number of hides of land in each hundred. The sheriff of Nottinghamshire and Derbyshire was required to work with a clerk, a representative sent by the king, and two knights from each hundred to assess what level of tax should be paid. It was then the responsibility of the knights and the hundred's bailiff to collect the taxes and pay it to the sheriff.

Peak Forest
now known as
High Peak

Scarsdale

Wirksworth

Appletree

Morleston

Litchurch

Repton
and
Gresley

Domesday Derbyshire

During the Christmas festivities in 1085, King William gave orders that royal commissioners should travel around his realm to make a survey of landownership and possessions. Enquiry was to be made about who owned property during the time of King Edward the Confessor, who owned it now that William was on the throne, and how much it was worth. The survey was carried out in 1086.

William the Conqueror was the chief landowner, or tenant-in-chief, in Derbyshire. As well as two thirds of the borough of Derby, he held a total of twenty-one manors throughout the county. Edward the Confessor and his predecessors had claimed many of them – for example Wirksworth, Hope, Bakewell and Melbourne – because they were of strategic importance or because of their mineral wealth. Each of the manors sat at the heart of a group of outlaying *berewicks*, or farms. Ashford-in-the-Water, which was also royal domain, possessed twelve berewicks. As well as land, meadows and woodland the manor controlled a mill and a lead mine, but it was not as wealthy as Bakewell, which was the wealthiest manor in the Peak District.

The king held mineral claims over the lead ore at Wirksworth. In AD 874, when Repton Abbey was destroyed by the Vikings, its lead mining rights were taken under the control of the Danish King Ceolwulf (who died in AD 879) and had remained a Crown right ever since. In 1086, the lead mining and smelting industries were long-established. The royal manor at Matlock was an important mineral resource, its limestone hills gradually turning into a honeycomb as miners followed the veins of ore. The Domesday Book also recorded that Bakewell and Ashford paid their duties to the Crown, in part, with smelted lead.

William also took lands for himself that had belonged to King Harold's extended family, and another group of manors that were once the possessions of Earl Edwin of Mercia.

The former were spoils of war and the latter were confiscated by the Crown when the earl rebelled in 1068. These estates are listed in the Domesday Book as belonging to Edwin's father Earl Ælfgar, who died in 1062. Much of the earl's former property lay in the strategically important Trent Valley at Walton-upon-Trent, Newton Solney, close to the Staffordshire border, Repton and Weston-upon-Trent.

Who's Who in Domesday Derbyshire?

In addition to the king, fifteen other men were listed as tenants-in-chief. Most of the county's pre-conquest owners were dispossessed or became tenants of land they once owned.

Robert de Limesey, Bishop of Chester, held Draycott, Hopwell, the manor of Bupton in the parish of Longford 11 miles west of Derby, and land in Long Eaton. The bishop also held the manor of Sawley near Erewash, which boasted two churches. It had been in the hands of Lichfield's bishop since as early as the seventh century and would remain the Bishop of Lichfield's domain until the Reformation in 1536. De Limesey retained the manor when he was moved from Lichfield to become Bishop of Chester in 1075.

Leofric, Abbot of Burton Abbey held only six manors on behalf of the abbey in modern-day Derbyshire. The manor of Mickleover near Derby included farms at Littleover, Finerdern and Potluck. He also held Appleby, Caldwell, Stapenhill, Ticknall and Coton-in-the-Elms, all in the south of the county. In Derby, the king granted the abbey the income from two mills, three houses, 13 acres of meadowland and the right to appoint the priest at St Mary's Church, one of the six churches in the town.

Hugh d'Avranches, 1st Earl of Chester, who was also called Hugh the Fat or Hugh the Wolf because of his attacks on Wales, was one of the king's companions as well as part of his extended family. By 1071, Hugh, who had a reputation for extravagant living, was an earl holding almost all of Cheshire. His Derbyshire holdings were confined to four manors, including Markeaton on the outskirts of Derby. He also acquired Kniveton, Mackworth and Allestree. During the 1070s he claimed one third of Derby's revenue for himself. This 'third penny' tax was later claimed by the Ferrers earls of Derby.

Hugh's son, Richard, drowned on the *White Ship* in 1120, along with King Henry I's only legitimate male heir. Hugh's estates and titles passed into the hands of a cousin. When the male line ended in 1237, the Crown took the opportunity to annex the earl's property for itself where it remained until the death of Edward, 'the Black Prince', in 1376.

Roger de Poitou, the fourth surviving son of Roger de Montgomery, Earl of Shrewsbury, who received the entire county of Lancashire comprising six hundreds, was granted eight manors in the north-east of Derbyshire in the Scarsdale hundred, which were held before the conquest by a man named Steinulf. He also held the manor of South Wingfield. When Roger rebelled against the king in 1086, the Crown reclaimed his estates almost before the ink in the Domesday Book was dry. Two years later, Roger was restored to his domain by King William II, better known as William Rufus, but when he rebelled against King Henry I in 1102, he was banished from England and stripped of his possessions.

Henry de Ferrers was the largest landowner in Derbyshire, holding more than 150 manors, which included the whole of the hundred of Appletree. Following a revolt in 1070–71, which he helped to suppress, de Ferrers was awarded the lands of Siward Bearn, who joined the rebellion of Hereward the Wake at Ely in East Anglia.

De Ferrers built a castle at Duffield to control the River Derwent's crossing point there. He also constructed fortifications to control the fording points and tracks at the upper end of the Dove Valley. When he died, sometime after 1093, de Ferrers' eldest son, William, inherited his estates in Normandy. De Ferrers intended for his second son, Engenulf, who was keeper of Duffield Castle, to inherit the estates granted to him by the Conqueror in England. However, Engenulf died before de Ferrers so it was Robert, the third of Henry's brood of sons, who inherited the estates in Derbyshire as well as his father's lead mining interests in the county, and who became the 1st Earl of Derby.

William Peveril was so much a favourite of William the Conqueror that people whispered that he was an illegitimate son of the king and that his mother, Maud, was the daughter of a Saxon prince. He was granted 162 manors, which formed the Honour of Peveril in Nottinghamshire and Derbyshire. As well as Castleton, Hucklow and Bradwell in the Peak District, he held Bolsover, Codnor and Pinxton, which lay on the border between the two counties.

Walter d'Aincourt, or Deincourt as it later became, was another royal kinsman. His lands lay mostly in Lincolnshire and Nottinghamshire but he possessed six manors in Derbyshire for which he owed the service of forty knights. The male line of his family ended in 1422 with the death of Walter Deincourt. His sisters became co-heiresses and the Derbyshire manors were divided between their husbands. Margaret Deincourt married Ralph, Lord Cromwell of Tattershall. Margaret's share included the manor of North Wingfield, where Cromwell, who was King Henry VI's Treasurer of the Exchequer, chose to build Wingfield Manor around two court-yards with a five-storey tower. The house was still incomplete when Cromwell died in 1455, and it passed on to the 2nd Earl of Shrewsbury, who had purchased it on the understanding that it would become his upon Cromwell's death.

The other sister, Alice, married William, Lord Lovell of Minster Lovell in Oxfordshire. Her grandson Francis, Viscount Lovell, was attainted of treason after the Battle of Bosworth in 1485 and his lands, along with the remains of the Deincourt inheritance at Holmesfield and Elmton, fell into the hands of the Manners and Rodes families, both long-established members of the Derbyshire gentry by the fifteenth century.

Geoffrey Alselin, who was an associate of Henry de Ferrers, acquired lands across the Midlands that, before the conquest, belonged to Toki, son of Auti, a wealthy thegn from Lincolnshire. Toki is thought to have been one of Hereward the Wake's companions. There is a possibility that Alselin fought against Hereward and was rewarded afterwards with land that belonged to the rebels. Alselin's manors in Derbyshire included Breaston, Elvaston, Ednaston, Etwall, Egginton, Ockbrook, Hollington and Hulland.

The Alselins retained their holdings until they passed through marriage into the Bardolf family. Elvaston later came into the hands of the Blounts, before finally being granted by King Henry VIII to Sir Michael Stanhope, whose good fortune ended in 1552 when he was beheaded for treason.

Ralph Fitz Hubert, the eldest son of the Lord of Ryes near Bayeux, was granted estates in the East Midlands that included at least forty-one manors in Derbyshire. He chose to make his caput at Crich, which offered him access to his manors in the north-east of Derbyshire at Eckington, Barlborough, Whitwell and Clowne.

Ralph de Burun held ten manors, or a significant part of them, in Derbyshire. He made Horsley near Derby his chief residence. Hugh's son, Roger, died without male heirs of his own. The land granted to Ralph became subject to a legal dispute between the descendants of Roger's sisters. Among them were the Byron family of whom the poet, Lord Byron, was one.

Hascoit Musard was from Brittany and served the king in the Breton section of his army at Hastings. He is associated with eight manors in Derbyshire, all in the vicinity of Chesterfield. He made his home a motte and bailey castle, at Staveley, which had a church, a mill, 60 acres of meadows and woodland pasture. His family continued to live there until the male line failed during the thirteenth century when Nicholas Musard died leaving three sisters as co-heiresses to the family's estates.

Gibert de Ghent, related to William the Conqueror's wife Matilda, was one of the commanders sent to York in 1067 to secure the city. He was still there in 1069 when its inhabitants, with the aid of a Danish fleet, rebelled against their new overlords. De Ghent is recorded as one of the few Normans spared from the flames and slaughter. He is associated with the title of 172 manors and lordships across the country. His possessions in Derbyshire lay in the south-east of the county at Ilkeston, West Hallam, Little Hallam, Stanton-by-Dale, Breaston and Shipley.

Nigel de Stafford's estates also lay in the south of Derbyshire. Changes to county boundaries mean that five of his eleven manors are no longer part of Derbyshire. Nigel's eldest son built a castle at Gresley and possibly a second one at Drakelow. By the twentieth century the Gresley family was unique among the landowners of Derbyshire for their possession, as tenant-in-chiefs, of land bestowed on them by William the Conqueror.

Robert Fitz William held the manor at Stanley but little else is known about him.

Roger de Busli, or de Bully, held 205 manors across the Midlands and Yorkshire. Many of the lands he was given had previously been held by Edwin, Earl of Mercia. De Busli was the largest landowner listed in the Domesday Book for Nottinghamshire, but he also held nine manors in the north-east of Derbyshire, in Scarsdale hundred.

PEVERIL OF THE PEAK

Soon after the conquest, William Peveril was made bailiff of the royal manors in the north-west of Derbyshire. Peveril Castle, one of the earliest stone castles in the country and the only castle identified in Derbyshire in 1086, overlooked the Hope Valley, where there was another motte and bailey fortification protecting the ford at Peakshole Water, which lay on the Roman road to Glossop.

Peveril's ambitions for his castle included building a town at Castleton planned on a grid and with a ditch for protection. The family also provided the area with a hospital, probably before 1150, north-west of Castleton called The Hospital of St Mary in the Peak, which was for the care of the sick and the poor.

DERBYSHIRE'S CASTLES

In the White Peak, soon after the conquest, Henry de Ferrers built fortifications at the upper end of Dove Dale to guard the river crossings and trackways there. There is evidence of motte and bailey fortifications at Pilsbury, Hartington at Bank Top, and it is now thought also at nearby Crowdecote. It is unclear why the cluster was established but it has been suggested that it was so that de Ferrers could safeguard his territory from the earls of Chester, whose lands marched with his, or else to levy taxes from the salt traders using paths across his land between Cheshire and Yorkshire. Of the three sites, only the earthworks at Pilsbury remain as an immediately recognisable feature in the landscape.

Further south, de Ferrers built a motte and bailey castle at Duffield. Henry's son Robert extended it to become the third largest fortification in England after the Tower and Dover Castle. The cost forced him to lease the mines he held at Wirksworth in 1130 to pay for the building works.

A CHURCH FIT FOR A KING

At Melbourne, in the south of the county, the Saxon church was replaced with an imposing new building made from stone from about 1136 to 1156. At the time, Adelulf, Bishop of Carlisle, lived and worshipped here from 1133 because Carlisle was either too dangerous or, from 1136 onwards, in the possession of the Scots.

Some people think that Melbourne Church was built by Adelulf to be a miniature cathedral because the church is so grand. Another, more likely, theory is that Melbourne was a royal manor and that the church was built on the orders of King Henry I. It has three towers. Inside, it has a crossing tower, an open gallery at its west end and upper-storey walkways. It also has an upper chancel at its east end, making it unique as a parish church. The gallery might be described as a royal pew, while the upper chancel fulfilled the function of private chapel.

As well as massive Norman columns, fine mouldings and rows of windows, there are many beautiful carvings inside the church. They include a grinning cat on one side of the chancel that appears to be mocking the dog carved opposite it, which is being held by its tail; a naked woman called a Sheela-na-gig, who was a symbol of fertility; and a Green Man with foliage sprouting from his mouth. It is not clear what the Green Man represented in medieval minds. To some people they are linked with pagan symbols of fertility, while others believe that the Green Man was used to represent changing seasons and rebirth.

THE ANARCHY IN DERBYSHIRE

The number of Derbyshire's fortifications grew during the civil war between King Stephen and the Empress Matilda, which took place between 1138 and 1153. Barons took the opportunity to expand their landholdings and indulge in feuds of their own as the national power struggle took a more local turn. Bolsover, granted to William Peveril by the Conqueror, was strengthened during this period. William de Gresley, the

eldest son of Nigel de Stafford, built a defensive structure at
Castle Gresley, while the de Buruns built a castle at Horsley in
the Amber Valley, overlooking the Derwent Valley.

In 1138, Robert de Ferrers, a prominent supporter of the king,
took a band of men from Derbyshire north to fight the Scots
and was present at the Battle of the Standard in Yorkshire. His
loyalty was rewarded by King Stephen, who made him 1st Earl
of Derbyshire. He was succeeded by his son, who became the
2nd Earl, the following year. The new earl continued to support
the king, but in 1153 was besieged at Tutbury in Staffordshire
by the future Henry II and changed sides.

The Peverils also supported King Stephen against the
Empress Matilda. When the empress's son Henry, who later
became King Henry II, sought support from powerful barons
to back his own bid for the throne in 1153, he offered Peveril's
land in Derbyshire to Ranulf de Gernon, the land-hungry 4th
Earl of Chester. Ranulf and Peveril were old adversaries.

That year, while the earl was Peveril's guest, he became
unwell, dying in December 1153. It was said that William
poisoned him. When Henry became king in 1154, William
Peveril was exiled and his estates confiscated. The forfeiture
of the Honour of Peveril to the Crown provided King Henry II
with the castles at Bolsover and Castleton and vast landholdings in Derbyshire.

In reality, Henry was punishing Peveril for his support of
King Stephen rather than for Ranulf's death. Peveril did not
have any sons who might have rebelled against the loss of
their inheritance. William and his wife, Avicia, had a daughter called Margaret who was married to the 2nd Earl of
Derbyshire, in about 1135, binding the two most important
families in Derbyshire at that time together. Henry II did not
entirely trust de Ferrers even though he gave the king his oath
of loyalty. The king refused to allow him to use the title of
earl and withdrew his rights to receive 'third penny' taxation
granted to the family by King Stephen.

3

MEDIEVAL DERBYSHIRE

Peveril Castle, at Castleton, stamped William Peveril's authority on the Peak Forest, which covered more than half the county, including the north-west of Derbyshire. The area was now the property of the king, and animals including deer and boar were reserved for the Crown. A carved tympanum, a semicircular decorative space above a door, at the church in Ashford-in-the-Water, a royal manor, portrays a boar and a wolf. Henry II, like the Norman kings before him, was passionate about hunting. It's known that he stayed at Peveril Castle in 1157 when Malcolm IV of Scotland came there to pay homage to the English king. Henry visited on at least two other occasions, in 1158 and 1164. He even sent two wolf trappers from the Peak Forest to catch wolves on his estates in Normandy in 1167.

The royal forest in Derbyshire was extended during the reign of King Henry II to include an area from the River Derwent to the Erewash. The region was not all wooded. Kinder Scout was an empty 'wasteland' – while other parts of the forest were used for farming and extended into manors owned by the Crown. As well as enjoying hunting, the forest provided timber and food as well as much-needed revenues, as the king was able to levy additional taxes on the people who lived in the forest areas.

Forest laws were ruthless. Men who possessed land under the jurisdiction of a Royal Forest were not allowed to hunt or to cut down trees. There were even rules about pannage, which was when farmers were able to release their pigs into the forest to feed on fallen acorns and nuts. Forest courts or 'eyres' that administered forest law were held at Glossop, Charlesworth, Tideswell and Chapel-en-le-Frith. Anyone hunting without royal permission could be blinded or maimed, although in practice offenders were usually fined.

Officials under the control of a chief forester upheld the law and collected rents and fines. Many of the offices were passed through the same family. The Woodroffes of Hope were wood-reeves, or forest stewards, for several generations. The church at Chapel-en-le-Frith, dedicated to St Thomas Becket, was built by foresters in 1225 to save them from having to travel to the parish church in Hope. Even today the church at Hope is noticeable for the number of memorials depicting axes, arrows and hunting horns associated with forest office.

THE MANOR SYSTEM

Derbyshire life was organised around the medieval manor system. It was the responsibility of the overlord to protect his tenants and to maintain order. In return they offered labour and, on occasion, military service. The men and women who lived and worked on a manor were tied through kinship, service and feudal obligation to one another and their over-lord. It was through the manorial system that resources were exploited, law and order enforced, and society regulated. A manor was a self-sufficient economy, often including a mill to make flour and a church as well as a village and manor house for the overlord or his steward.

The removal of the Peverils and the de Ferrer earls of Derby and the substitution of absentee crown landlords left a void in the medieval social hierarchy.

Even so, manor houses sprang up throughout the county. The Old Manor at Norbury near Ashbourne, a seat of the Fitzherbert family, is an example of a hall house built in about 1290. Fenny Bentley, in the Peak District, retains a tower from its fifteenth-century manor house. Outside Bakewell, at Haddon, Richard Vernon was granted permission by King John to build a curtain wall around his home. The battle-mented and turreted building sitting above the River Wye is regarded as one of the finest medieval houses in the country.

THE OPEN FIELD SYSTEM

Each manor had two or three large fields that were divided into narrow strips of land. These strips were farmed by dif-ferent tenants. The method left long lines of parallel ridges and furrows in the ground where the land was ploughed. The ghost of this system of cultivation can be seen in fields across Derbyshire; for example, at Brassington in the Peak District and at Chaddesdon Park near Derby. In return for land, the lord of the manor received rent from freemen who made up about 12 per cent of the population. The rest of the agricul-tural labourers, known as villeins or serfs, were not free. They worked three days a week on the lord's land before they could look after their own crops.

PINFOLDS

Each manor possessed areas of common land where tenants had a right to graze their animals. Pinfold enclosures were used to hold animals that were found grazing on common land without their owner's right to do so, or if they strayed onto land where they should not have been. Animals were kept in the pinfold until a fine was paid, which also included the cost of caring for them. The system was administered by an official called a pinder. By the sixteenth century most villages had one. Hope, Birchover and Curbar are among the villages that still retain their pounds. They vary in date and condition.

PEDLARS AND PILGRIMS

Pedlars used routes such as the Long Causey at Hathersage, as well as old Roman roads and prehistoric trackways. The pack ponies that traders led often carried salt from mines in Cheshire to Sheffield. By the end of the era, the county was criss-crossed with paths. Some Peak District routes across the moors were so well trodden that they formed sunken lanes or hollow ways. The one running between Lea and Upper Holloway in the Amber Valley, which leads up to the moor there, gives the village its name. Clapper bridges like the ones at Baslow and Youlgreave were built from large foundation blocks with rectangular stones laid over them to make water crossings easier.

Other travellers included pilgrims visiting local shrines. A carved figure at the church in Youlgreave depicts a pilgrim with a satchel and staff. St Alkmund's, whose body was returned to Derby in about 1140 from Shrewsbury, was a popular place to visit, as was Repton Priory, which possessed St Guthlac's bell, said to provide a cure for headaches.

MONASTIC DERBYSHIRE

Calke Priory near Ticknell was founded by Richard d'Avranches, 2nd Earl of Chester, as a house for Augustinian canons soon after the Norman Conquest. Augustinians followed monastic rules but they were not an enclosed order. Many of them continued to work in the wider community as ordained priests. In 1153, the canons were granted St Wystan's Church in Repton by Maud, Countess of Chester, when her husband Ranulf died. In 1172, by which time a new priory was completed at Repton, the majority of Calke's canons transferred to it, fulfilling an obligation imposed by Maud.

In about 1154, Robert Ferrers, 2nd Earl of Derby, with King Henry II's agreement, founded the Augustinian Priory of St Mary at Darley, 2 miles north of Derby. Other landowners were quick to offer their own gifts, including the right to appoint the priest at eight churches across Derbyshire. At Ripley, the canons held the manor and the right to hold a market and a fair there. By 1291 their annual income was £72 19*s* 3½*d*.

In about 1160, the abbot at Darley recognised that there was a need to establish a nunnery in Derbyshire. He set up a Benedictine convent at King's Mead in Derby, just a mile from the priory. A small house was provided for a warden appointed to act as the nun's chaplain and to look after business matters. In 1229, King Henry III granted the nuns land so that they could pasture their flocks. He also ordered that £5 a year should be paid from his rents in Nottingham so that the nuns could pray for the soul of his father, King John. Kingsmead was the only nunnery in Derbyshire, and by 1250 it operated independently from Darley Abbey. It became a popular place for the local elite to send their daughters to be educated as well as a place where they might enter holy orders.

Several other monastic houses were founded in or near Derby during the twelfth and thirteenth centuries. William de Gresley founded another Augustinian priory on his land at Gresley. The Curzons became patrons of the priory at Breadsall. It was never a wealthy house, and always struggled with poverty despite donations from local families. When Thomas Cromwell's commissioners visited it in 1535, before the dissolution of the monasteries, they found that William Pendleton, the prior, was the only canon left and that the priory's annual income was only £10 17s 9d. The Premonstratensian abbey at Dale near Ilkeston was subject to several false starts before it gained enough land and support to flourish in 1204. The monks who built their house on the site of an old hermitage received grants of land from the FitzRalph and de Grendon families at Ockbrook, Sandiacre and Alvaston, as well as a mill at Borrowash, near Spondon.

The men and women who founded monastic houses and gifted them property or rights expected the monks and nuns to pray for the souls of the patrons and their families forever. It was thought that prayer was a way of helping people to reduce the amount of time they spent in Purgatory paying for their sins before going to Heaven.

MONASTIC FARMS

In the Peak District, a monastic presence was experienced in the form of farms owned by abbeys and priories called granges. Worked by lay brothers and paid servants, the granges were mostly sheep farms selling their wool in Ashbourne, Hartington and Chesterfield.

From the time of the Norman Conquest onwards, Derbyshire landholders showed their devotion to God, and hoped for their sins to be pardoned, by becoming the patrons of religious houses. This often involved the gift of land. More than thirty monasteries across the Midlands, and beyond, owned property in Derbyshire.

The Peveril family granted manors, including Tideswell, to Lenton Priory in Nottinghamshire, which they founded during the twelfth century. The monks there gave their name to Monk's Dale, although not much else remains. Bradbourne in the Peak District was held in 1205 by Geoffrey de Caucis, who granted the living of the church and the manor to the Augustinians of Dunstable Priory in Bedfordshire to support its hospice, which cared for travellers. The chapels of Ballidon, Brassington, Tissington and Atlow were included in the gift, which was confirmed by the 4th Earl of Derby in 1222. One Ash Grange near Monyash was both a sheep farm and a place of punishment for the monks of Roche Abbey in South Yorkshire.

THE GROWTH OF CHESTERFIELD
AND DERBYSHIRE'S MARKETS

By the twelfth century, Chesterfield, in north-east Derbyshire, was a town rather than a village. King John's charter of 1204 permitted the town the same rights as Derby and Nottingham, including a market twice a week as well as an annual eight-day fair.

He also granted the whole of the hundred of Scarsdale, of which Chesterfield was a part, to William Brewer or Briwere, who was sheriff of Nottingham and Derbyshire until 1200. Brewer developed Chesterfield's economy by building a large marketplace laid out west of the church, together with tenements on either side of the space. The shambles, where butchers traded, dates back to the same time.

In 1203, Hartington was the first of Derbyshire's villages to receive its market charter. It was granted to William de Ferrers, 4th Earl of Derby, who was something of a favourite of King John's. Markets and fairs attracted buyers and sellers from a wide area, and added to a village or town's revenue as well as the fees of the men who held manor rights in those locations.

Wirksworth and Bakewell were granted their market charters, and the right to hold an annual fair, together with Ashbourne, Alfreton, Bolsover, Ilkeston, Ripley and Melbourne during the thirteenth century. In time, many of the places, especially those to the east of the county, were granted a medieval market charter and grew into towns.

KING JOHN IN DERBYSHIRE

In 1189, Richard I gave the Honour of Peveril to his brother, Prince John. In 1192, John gifted Bakewell Minster to the Dean and Chapter of Lichfield, in return for which the new priest was to pray for the prince's health and safety during his lifetime and for his soul after his death. The grant resulted in a violent disagreement followed by a court case in Rome between Lichfield and Lenton Priory, near Nottingham. The latter claimed that their founder, William Peveril, gave them the tithes at Bakewell. Pope Celestine III ruled that the tithes, a tax totalling one tenth of Bakewell's annual income, were rightfully Lenton's, but that the priory should make an annual payment to Lichfield from the proceeds. It did not help that the charter used to confirm Peveril's gifts to the priory was a forgery.

In 1204, King John lost his domains in Normandy to the French. He became obsessed with winning them back. It was essential to levy all the taxes that were available to him so that he could raise an army. The burden fell heavily on people who lived and worked in Derbyshire's royal forests.

Baronial opposition to John's high-handed approach to taxation led to a northern plot against him in 1212. That winter John shored up his defences, including at Bolsover, which offered some control of the road south. He also tried to increase his revenues by selling charters that lifted some of the constraints imposed by forest law. William FitzWakelin of Stainsby near Chesterfield and Hubert FitzRalph of Crich were among the men who paid for the right to fell trees and hunt as they pleased within their own manors.

By 1215, civil war seemed inevitable. John is known to have visited his deer park at Melbourne at the end of March on his way from Nottingham to Lichfield. Like his predecessors, he spent much time in Derbyshire hunting. He was due to meet with his barons less than a month later at Northampton to discuss the liberties they demanded. It was June before he finally met with them at Runnymede and signed the Magna Carta. The Sheriff of Nottinghamshire and Derbyshire, Philip Mark, was so widely reviled for implementing the king's policies that the barons demanded his removal from office and wrote it into the charter.

Unrest erupted into open warfare when John went back on the agreement that, in future, kings would be accountable to the rule of law. William de Ferrers, 4th Earl of Derby, held the castles at Bolsover and Castleton on behalf of the king, and was made bailiff of the Peak Forest as well as warden of Peveril Castle. In face of the threat presented by men like John Deincourt of Morton and Ralph de Willoughby of Glapwell, who supported the barons' demands, the earl also fortified Horsley Castle in the Amber Valley.

In 1216, shortly before his death, King John is thought to have confirmed the rights that he first granted to Derby's burgesses in 1204. As well as holding a weekly market, the burgesses were permitted to levy tolls from traders and punish thieves. However, it was John's son, King Henry III, who granted the town its first written charter in 1229, which not only included the right to hold a weekly market but also forbade the sale of cloth within 30 miles of Derby except at Nottingham.

THE BATTLE OF CHESTERFIELD
AND THE DESTRUCTION OF DUFFIELD CASTLE

The Earl of Derby was permitted to retain control over Bolsover, Peveril Castle and Horsley during the minority of John's son, King Henry III. In 1222, the king celebrated his fourteenth birthday and became old enough to rule in his own right. To de Ferrers' irritation, the three royal castles were reclaimed for the king.

In 1247, William succeeded his father as 5th Earl of Derby, but he died in 1254 leaving a young son, Robert, to inherit the earldom. That same year the three royal castles in Derbyshire were granted to Henry III's son Edward, who also became Robert de Ferrer's guardian for a brief time before selling the young earl's wardship to his uncle, Peter of Savoy, for 6,000 marks. It was the start of the 6th Earl of Derby's festering resentment against Prince Edward.

By 1264, the king and his barons were at war with one another once again, because Henry III also reneged on the agreement made by Magna Carta that sought to establish royal accountability. Robert de Ferrers supported Simon de Montfort and the rebel barons. The origin of de Ferrers' support for the barons had less to do with the king's high-handed attitude than a personal dislike of Prince Edward. De Ferrers also held a lingering family grudge relating to the ownership of Peveril Castle. He believed it should be his by right of the marriage the 2nd Earl made to Margaret Peveril. By the end of 1264, the earl was in possession of the castles of Bolsover, Horsley and Peveril.

Many of the barons felt that Simon de Montfort went too far when he captured the king and Prince Edward, placing them under house arrest after the Battle of Lewes in Sussex in May 1264. De Montfort decided that to regain the barons' support, Edward should be released and his possessions returned to him. When de Ferrers refused to return the prince's Derbyshire castles and estates, de Montfort had the earl arrested and imprisoned in the Tower.

As a result of his imprisonment, de Ferrers was absent from the rebel ranks when Edward escaped captivity and defeated de Montfort at the Battle of Evesham on 4 August 1265. Henry III, who needed de Ferrers' support in the Midlands, released the earl in November 1265. His lands and position were restored to him upon payment of a large fine.

Within five months of making them, the Earl of Derby broke his oath to the king. He joined with Baldwin Wake, Lord of Chesterfield, who inherited the manor in 1233 through mar-

riage to Isabel, daughter of William Brewer. The pair marched from Duffield Castle with an army to Chesterfield on 15 May, pursued by a royalist army led by Henry III's nephew, Henry of Almain.

The king's army circled Chesterfield and attacked John D'Ayville of Hode Castle in Yorkshire north of the town, at Dronfield, to prevent him from joining with the earl. Weakened by the assault, D'Ayville retreated, leaving the earl and Wake to face the royalists. Chesterfield had a defensive town ditch and a wooden rampart but the rebels were taken by surprise. In the confusion that followed, many lesser barons and knights from Derbyshire were either killed or taken prisoner, while others, including Wake, escaped. Henry of Almain secured Chesterfield for the king and then began searching for de Ferrers. He threatened to burn the town to the ground unless the whereabouts of the earl was revealed. The 29-year-old was eventually discovered hiding in, or near, the church.

At Windsor Castle, the 6th Earl was found guilty of treason. His life was spared but he was forced to agree to pay a fine valued at seven times his annual income in return for his freedom. His possessions were seized and Duffield Castle, reputedly the third largest Norman keep in the country, was razed to the ground. The king gave the earl's estates to his own younger son, Edmund, Earl of Lancaster. His heirs, the Dukes of Lancaster, would have significant influence over Derbyshire and its inhabitants during the fourteenth and fifteenth centuries.

LEAD MINING

Lead mining continued to flourish in the county, providing Derbyshire's landowners and the Crown with mineral wealth. The Odin Mine at Castleton was in operation throughout the medieval period. Lead from Derbyshire was used for King Henry II's building works at Windsor and Winchester, as well as by Henry III when lead from Wirksworth was used to re-roof Westminster Abbey. By the second half of the thirteenth century, Derbyshire dominated the English lead industry.

In 1288, King Edward I regularised the laws controlling lead mining when he visited Ashbourne. He ordered the establishment of barmote courts to be composed of twenty-four jurors. Each court was run by a barmaster and steward whose job was to grant title of ownership to a mine, or groove, once a miner showed that there was workable ore; to settle property disputes; withdraw title if a mine was left unworked; explore the causes of any sudden deaths of miners; to measure the lead ore; and to collect mineral duties known as 'lot and cope'. The first dish of ore, or 'lot', from a vein, or 'rake', was payable to the landowner. A dish weighed 29kg. Once barmote officials staked out the ground around the miner's claim the title of the mine was theirs to work unhindered. The Crown made a claim on every thirteenth lot of ore. A duty known as 'cope' was to be paid by the merchants purchasing the ore from the miners. In Wirksworth, where a court is still held, miners were required to pay every fortieth dish they mined as a tithe to the Church.

BRIDGING THE TRENT

A bridge was first mentioned at Swarkestone in 1204, but in 1276 it was replaced by a more durable stone structure. It improved Derby's transport links with the important medieval town of Coventry and was the only bridging point between Burton and Nottingham. The bridge was almost a mile in length, because after crossing the river it turned into a raised causeway across the Trent Valley's low-lying floodplain. Even today the oldest parts of it date to the thirteenth century, and it remains England's longest stone bridge.

Merchants were quick to make use of the new facilities, but they were required to pay a toll. At first this income was granted to the borough of Derby, but in 1325, King Edward II, who was visiting Melbourne, reallocated the toll so that the bridge could be kept in good repair.

THE REAL ROBIN HOOD?

James Coterel and his brothers were racketeers, extortionists and murderers. They first came to the attention of the authorities in 1328, when they attacked and beat up the vicar of Bakewell at the instigation of a former vicar, Robert Bernard. He had been removed from his post when he was found to have stolen from church funds. When the Coterels failed to appear in court to answer the charges against them, they were outlawed. The gang took to the forest, where they continued to receive rents from their lands and to recruit new members. They were supported by several churchmen, including the dean and chapter of Lichfield Cathedral as well as several local knights. Roger de Wennesley, Lord of Mappleton, joined them rather than bringing them to justice. Even Sir Robert Ingram, the Sheriff of Nottingham and Derbyshire, was an ally of theirs.

In 1332, Richard de Willoughby, an unpopular Justice of the Peace from Nottinghamshire, was sent to bring the gang to justice. The Coterels turned the tables on Willoughby when they kidnapped and ransomed him for 1,300 marks. King Edward III was so incensed by their lawlessness that he sent a royal commission to Derbyshire to restore order. The gang was arraigned, but the Coterel brothers ignored the summons. Not that it mattered: all but one man was acquitted when their case came to trial. The outbreak of war with Scotland in the same year presented a solution to the king's problem. He pardoned the Coterels in return for payment of a substantial fine and recruited them into his army.

THE BLACK DEATH

The bubonic plague, known as the Black Death, arrived in England in 1348. The disease wiped out between a quarter and a third of England's total population. It is believed to have arrived in Derbyshire in May 1349 and spared neither the urban populations of Derby and Chesterfield nor the more remote upland districts. Depopulation resulted in the medieval villages of Osleston and Meynell Langley being deserted. The loss of peasant labour resulted in a rise in wages that weakened society's feudal bonds. Families moved to other villages or towns in search of better pay and conditions in the years following the plague's arrival.

In Chesterfield, building work on St Mary and All Saints' parish church was interrupted when skilled masons and carpenters died from the pestilence.

The spire, made from unseasoned wood and without cross bracing inside the structure, was added to the church in about 1362 by unskilled workmen, who did not understand that as the timber dried it would warp. It means that today the county's largest parish church has a spire twisted at 45 degrees and leaning approximately 2.5m from its true centre.

CHELLASTON MARBLE

At around the same time, masons began to use a marble-like form of gypsum, a sulphate of lime, called 'alabaster' that was quarried from Chellaston, a few miles south of Derby, to create effigies on tombs and for statues. When the stone emerges from the ground it is soft and easy to work but it hardens after exposure to the air. When polished, it looks like marble. Chellaston marble was used extensively for the next 300 years.

Some of the finest examples in the country are the Fitzherbert tombs at Norbury, dating from the end of the fifteenth century, which were once richly coloured and gilded. One of the most unusual examples can be found in the church at Fenny Bentley where Thomas Beresford, a commander at Agincourt, and his wife were buried. Their effigies, created sometime after their deaths, when the mason did not know what they looked like, depict them in their shrouds, which are tied in knots on the tops of their heads.

THE DUCHY OF LANCASTER, JOHN OF GAUNT AND THE LANDOWNERS OF DERBYSHIRE

Lancastrian landholdings in Derbyshire were extended through marriage, inheritance and royal grant. In 1362, the Duchy of Lancaster was bestowed on John of Gaunt, the third surviving son of King Edward III, by right of his marriage to Blanche of Lancaster, the daughter of Henry of Grosmont, 1st Duke of Lancaster, who was descended from King Henry III's younger son, Edmund.

In 1372, John of Gaunt, Duke of Lancaster, exchanged estates in Hertfordshire for the castle and manor at Castleton so that he could consolidate his power in the Midlands. Gaunt's position in Derbyshire as a noble landowner was a unique one. The Greys of Codnor were of minor importance even though they were part of the peerage. The duke's authority ensured that landowners of the middle rank who owed their allegiance to him were regularly returned to the offices of sheriff, Justice of the Peace, members of parliament and Peak Forest officials. By the 1390s, several families from Derbyshire were part of the Duke and Duchess of Lancaster's household, while others were in service in the royal household. Sir Walter Blount of Barton Blount was notably successful in raising the status and fortunes of his family thanks to the patronage of John of Gaunt.

These middling landowners, of whom there were approximately thirty families in Derbyshire, emerged in the fifteenth century as the gentry. They were bound to the House of Lancaster and one another by kinship, and the opportunities that presented themselves through service in return for advancement.

POLL TAXES, REVOLTING PEASANTS
AND THE RISE OF THE HOUSE OF LANCASTER

In 1377, a poll tax was levied on every man and woman in the country. Only children under the age of 14 were exempt from payment. A total of 24,289 people in Derbyshire were eligible to pay, and 456 monks and nuns were taxed separately. The levying of a second tax in 1380, followed by a third tax in 1381, sparked the Peasants' Revolt. In Derbyshire, rebels murdered Henry Massy, a supporter of John of Gaunt, at his home at Morley in Erewash. They burned Breadsall Priory to the ground and seized Horsley Castle.

In 1399, King Richard II was deposed by his cousin Henry of Bolingbroke, who had been banished from England in 1398. He returned home following the death of his father, John of Gaunt, claiming that he sought only his rightful inheritance. Men from Derbyshire were mostly loyal to the House of Lancaster. They were well rewarded when Henry became King Henry IV. Sir Hugh Shirley gained the constableship of Castle Donington, while Sir John Cokayne was granted the town of Ashbourne, worth £60 a year.

Derbyshire's gentry continued to serve the Lancastrian kings of England. They were part of Henry V's army that waged the Hundred Years' War against France. In 1415, many of them fought at Agincourt. Richard, Lord Grey of Codnor, commanded a band of 222 tenants. Another group was led by Philip Leach of Chatsworth, while a third troop was commanded by Thomas Beresford, whose achievement was recorded on his monument at Fenny Bentley. The Crispin Inn at Ashover is thought to have been named in honour of the victory. Local landowner Thomas Babington of Dethick was among the men from Derbyshire who returned from the battle.

LAWLESSNESS IN DERBYSHIRE
AND THE WARS OF THE ROSES

King Henry VI became king when he was only 9 months old in 1422. A regency council ruled on his behalf for the next fifteen years. In Derbyshire, law and order began to break down as men used the opportunity to indulge in private feuds. On 1 January 1434, Henry Longford and William Bradshawe were murdered during a church service at Chesterfield. A third man, Sir Henry Pierrepoint, was wounded. The killings arose from a dispute between Pierrepoint and Thomas Foljambe. An assault, originating in a territory dispute, had taken place on Foljambe the previous year.

Private feuds became more frequent as court factions supporting either the house of York or Lancaster warred with one another at a national level. Walter Blount, whose family was traditionally loyal to the House of Lancaster, switched his allegiance to Richard of York during the 1450s. It exacerbated a feud with the Longford family. In 1453, Thomas Blount, a younger son of Sir Thomas Blount, was waylaid and stabbed at Kingsmead in Derby. When a writ was served against Sir Nicholas Longford for his involvement in the crime, the royal messenger was assaulted and made to swallow the document together with its seal.

Richard, Duke of York, who was England's protector by then, summonsed the combatants before the royal council in 1454, but in Derbyshire he was not seen to be acting as a neutral. He was, in the eyes of the Longford family, a patron of Walter Blount. On 28 May, an army of Longford's supporters, including many of Derbyshire's most important families, attacked Blount's house in Derby. When the sheriff, Sir John Gresley, met them in the marketplace to try and persuade them to disband, they ignored him. Instead, they ransacked Blount's manor house at Elvaston, destroying his furniture and tearing up the hangings with his coat of arms on them into quarters, declaring that Blount was a traitor because he served Richard of York.

Blount's continued service to the House of York saw him weather the storms of the civil war between Lancaster and York, rising to become Baron Mountjoy and serving on the royal council. He was even permitted to marry Edward IV's widowed aunt, Anne, the Duchess of Buckingham, who possessed property in Derbyshire. Other men from the county also reconciled themselves to the Yorkists, including Nicholas Fitzherbert, whose effigy at Norbury near Ashbourne shows him wearing Edward IV's livery collar decorated with suns and roses.

WHO'S WHO IN DERBYSHIRE'S WARS OF THE ROSES?

The great nobles and barons who owned land in Derbyshire were non-resident. They employed local estate owners as bailiffs and stewards, as well as appointing them to regional offices. The growth of each magnate's influence in the county was based on patronage, kinship and local politics. The patterns of patronage meant that most of Derbyshire's smaller landowners, the gentry, were pragmatic about their support of Lancaster and York during the Wars of the Roses, because they wished to retain their lands and regional influence.

The most important landowner in Derbyshire was the Duchy of Lancaster, or the Crown once John of Gaunt's son became King Henry IV. The House of Lancaster had close ties to the county. Henry's title before he took Richard II's throne was Earl of Derby.

George, Duke of Clarence, was the brother of the Yorkist king, Edward IV. Edward granted Clarence estates in 1461 that were previously in the possession of the Duchy of Lancaster. The king's decision to give the property to Clarence was part of his strategy to ensure the future allegiance of Derbyshire landowners to the Yorkist line from which Edward and his brothers were descended, rather than to the Lancastrian branch of the royal family.

Clarence, resentful of the influence of Edward IV's wife, Elizabeth Woodville, and her family, joined with Richard Neville, Earl of Warwick, in rebellion against the king in 1469. It was only after his execution in 1478 that the duke's lands in Derbyshire were reassigned to Edward's chamberlain, William Hastings. He forfeited them, in 1483, when he was executed for treason by King Richard III. In 1485, the estates were resumed by the Crown when Henry Tudor, the Lancastrian claimant, became King Henry VII following his victory at the Battle of Bosworth.

Richard Neville, Earl of Warwick, inherited the lordship of Chesterfield by right of his mother, Alice Montacute, Countess of Salisbury, who was descended from the Holland earls of Kent. Richard II granted estates in Derbyshire, including Chesterfield, to his half-brother, John Holland, in an unsuccessful attempt to counter the power of the Dukes of Lancaster in the region at the end of the fourteenth century.

John Talbot, 1st Earl of Shrewsbury, became an earl in 1442 following a career as a military commander serving in France. The main seat of the family was Sheffield but John's first wife, Maud Furnival, brought several Derbyshire manors into Talbot's hands, including Eyam and Brassington. It was the start of a growing influence that would turn the family into important Tudor Derbyshire landowners. In 1483, the Talbot family joined with Henry Tudor at Newport as he advanced through the Midlands.

THE VERNONS OF HADDON HALL

The power of local landowning families fluctuated throughout the medieval period. Each Derbyshire hundred had its own dominant family and its own disputes. The Blount–Longford conflict was unusual because the Protectorate Council of Richard of York became involved with a regional conflict.

The Vernon family kept their political options open and ensured they were part of an extensive and influential kinship network. They began the period as part of the group of Derbyshire landowning gentry who held various offices under John of Gaunt, Henry IV and Henry V. They were unusual because their estates were more extensive than the rest of Derbyshire's landowners.

Sir Richard Vernon, like many other members of Derbyshire's leading families, served the Crown in France during the Hundred Years' War. In 1423, he was appointed steward for the Duchy of Lancaster in the High Peak. In 1426, he was elected as MP for Derbyshire and Speaker of the House of Commons. He died in 1451 and was succeeded by his son, Sir William, who inherited his father's estates and offices.

It was Sir William who negotiated the change in regime between Lancaster and York to the benefit of the Vernons in the aftermath of Edward IV's victory at Towton in 1461. Sir Henry Vernon, William's heir, rose under the Yorkist regime because of his allegiance to George, Duke of Clarence. He also made an expedient marriage to Anne Talbot, a daughter of the Earl of Shrewsbury, in 1466. When Clarence and his cousin the Earl of Warwick rebelled against Edward IV in 1469, Vernon was summoned to join them. Preferring to avoid the possibility of being found guilty of treason, he provided a series of excuses to avoid taking to the field for either side. By the middle of the 1470s, Sir Henry sat on Derbyshire peace commissions, and in 1478 became an MP. Edward IV described him as 'trusty and well beloved' in 1481 and appointed him to the post of Bailiff of the High

Peak. Vernon's hard-headed approach ensured that he was always able to demonstrate his loyalty to the Crown even though he may have harboured a personal allegiance to the Lancastrian cause.

By the time Henry VII came to the throne in 1485, the Vernon family had emerged as the region's dominant family. Given the favour that Henry VII showed to Sir Henry, it is likely that he was with the king at the Battle of Bosworth on 22 August 1485 in the company of the Earl of Shrewsbury. Vernon's standing in society, and wealth, is apparent from the scale of his building work at Haddon Hall.

4

TUDOR DERBYSHIRE
(1485–1603)

Sir Henry Vernon was appointed as governor and treasurer to Henry VII's eldest son, Prince Arthur, in 1487 as a reward for his support of the king. There is a room at Haddon Hall known as the Prince's Chamber because tradition states that the prince stayed there. When Arthur died in 1502, Vernon's political ambitions suffered. The blow was compounded when he kidnapped a local heiress, Margaret Kebell, and married her to his eldest son, Roger. Fortunately for the Vernons, although the king fined Sir Henry, he pardoned the family and they continued to prosper in their service to the Tudors. Sir George Vernon, Henry's grandson, was knighted at the coronation of King Edward VI and became so wealthy that he was known as the King of the Peak.

THE END OF THE MONASTERIES

By 1527, King Henry VIII, who had only one surviving legitimate daughter, was infatuated with Anne Boleyn and the promise of a male heir. Only the pope could annul the king's marriage to his first wife, Catherine of Aragon. Henry was certain, at first, that the papacy would grant him his desire. But with the passage of time, the king became convinced that he would never be free of Catherine, while the pope and the Catholic Church embodied by the monasteries retained control of ecclesiastical law.

By 1534, many religious houses were understandably nervous about what the future held. James Billingford, a disgraced priest from Suffolk, hit upon a plan to play upon these fears to defraud unwary nuns of their money. He travelled from town to town pretending to be Anne Boleyn's chaplain. He gained admittance to Kingsmead, where he persuaded the nuns while their abbess was away that he was required to make a report, and that he would either be favourable or bring about Kingsmead's closure. He was soon shown to be a fake. The prior at Darley provided Thomas Cromwell, the king's chief minister, with a statement about Billingford's behaviour.

In 1535, Cromwell sent his own commissioners to assess the wealth of the realm's monastic houses and uncover their scandals. The only item of note for Kingsmead was that the nuns possessed a relic alleged to be part of Thomas Becket's shirt that was venerated by the pregnant ladies of Derby. The following year Parliament passed an act closing all religious houses in England and Wales worth less than £200 per year. Despite being the only nunnery in Derbyshire, Kingsmead was not granted a stay of execution. All that remains of Kingsmead today is a reference to Nun's Street in Derby.

At Dale, the commissioners reported that the abbot was conducting affairs with two women while one of his canons, William Brampton, enjoyed relationships with five married women. Irrespective of the alleged mores of the canons, the abbey was granted, for a consideration of £166 13s 4d paid to the Court of Augmentations, an exemption from closure in 1536. Dale did not have long to enjoy its reprieve. On 24 October 1538, the abbot, prior and fifteen canons signed the deed of surrender to Sir William Cavendish, one of Cromwell's men. It ended almost four centuries of monastic life.

Cavendish gave orders for an army of workmen to remove the lead from the roof of Dale as soon as it was surrendered to him. Men knocked the keystones from the vaulted roof of the Lady Chapel and allowed the roof to smash into the tiled pavement beneath to make the abbey uninhabitable. All that remains of the thirteenth-century abbey is the 12m-high east window, while parts of the village church, rather unusually attached to a private house, date back to 1150 and the earliest days of monastic settlement on the site. Before the Reformation, the abbey's chapel adjoined its infirmary. After the dissolution of the monasteries, the infirmary became a pub and then a farm.

An unexpected consequence of the dissolution, which saw the end of every abbey and priory in the country with a Parliamentary Act passed in 1539, was the collapse in the price of Derbyshire's lead as the market was swamped by a flood of metal stripped from the roofs of all the monastic houses.

Altogether, Derbyshire monasteries were valued as having an annual income of £3,337 9s 6d. The gentry, who had previously been patrons of the very same foundations, were eager to benefit from the bonanza. A notable exception was the Fitzherbert family, who refused to profit from the end

of monasticism. At first the king intended to rent or lease the land he gained with the closure of Derbyshire's monasteries. The priory at Breadsall and its land was rented from the Crown by Lawrence Holland of Belper soon after its closure. At Darley, Robert Sacheverell, who was a younger son, improved his fortunes by selling the goods and fabric of the abbey. An agreement was in place between the Sacheverell and Pole families for both Dale and Darley before their priors surrendered their houses.

King Henry needed money to pay for his wars against Scotland and France, and decided to sell the majority of the land. At Dale, Sir Francis Pole of Radbourne took possession of the remains of the abbey, while at Darley, Sir William West built a manor on the site of the priory.

THE CAVENDISHES

The Cavendish family, newly arrived in sixteenth-century Derbyshire, came to dominate the region because of their extensive land acquisitions and judicious marriages. William Cavendish began his career as the younger son of a Suffolk landowner. However, as one of Cromwell's senior officials, it was Cavendish's task to visit the realm's monasteries to audit their accounts. Later he held an office in the Court of Augmentations that processed the sale of the abbeys. He accrued land and wealth at the same time. When Cavendish married Elizabeth Hardwick, better known as Bess of Hardwick, in 1547, he sold his estates elsewhere in the south of the country so that he could relocate to Derbyshire. One of the estates he purchased in 1549, on the advice of his wife, was at Chatsworth.

Bess and her husband both had a shrewd eye for business and began to accumulate land. In 1550, Henry Neville, Earl of Westmorland, sold them the manor of Ashford along with 8,000 acres of land. The estates remain in the hands of the pair's descendants, the Dukes of Devonshire, to this day. Among Cavendish's purchases across the Peak District was the village of Buxton and a coal mine at Pentrich.

By the end of 1553, Bess had provided her husband with three sons and the future of the family seemed secure. She built a magnificent new house at Chatsworth. Then, in the summer of 1553, Henry VIII's son, the young Edward VI, died. He was succeeded by his sister Mary, who was a staunch Catholic. Somehow Sir William Cavendish was able to survive the change in regime but was accused of fraud. For a time, Bess's husband faced imprisonment and the loss of Chatsworth. Only his timely death prevented disaster for the whole family.

MARY TUDOR (REIGNED 1553–58)

The divide between Catholics and Protestants became more pronounced during Mary's reign. The queen expected her subjects to return to the Catholic faith that her father, and particularly her brother, Edward VI, rejected.

In Derby, Joan Waste, a young woman blind from birth, had attended All Saints Church since childhood. Kindly parishioners would read portions of the Bible in English to her, which she memorised. When Mary became queen, it suddenly became dangerous for Joan's readers because the Catholic Church tried to turn the clock back and to ban Bibles written in English. By then Joan was a committed Protestant. The town's bailiffs tried to persuade the young woman to keep her views to herself. But when challenged by priests, she held firm to her beliefs and was arrested for heresy on the orders of the Bishop of Coventry and Lichfield. The bishop's chancellor, Dr Anthony Draycot, was sent to question her. Joan was kept in prison for a month but she refused to change her mind, even though she was told that she would be burned at the stake as a heretic.

On 1 August 1556, Joan was led from her prison cell to attend church, where Draycott preached a sermon to a congregation that included Sir Henry Vernon, himself a firm Protestant. Then Joan's twin brother led her to Windmill Pit on Burton Road, Derby, where she was executed.

QUEEN ELIZABETH I (REIGNED 1558–1603)

When Elizabeth became queen, all the clergy were required to take an oath recognising her as the Supreme Governor of the Church of England as the government returned to Protestantism. Twenty-nine men refused to take the oath at Derby on 19 September 1559. Sir Anthony Draycott, who condemned Joan Waste of heresy in 1556, was one of them. He was imprisoned and sent to London. A number of Derbyshire's gentry also refused to recognise Elizabeth as head of the Church in England. Some of these refusers, or 'recusants' as they were known, were prepared to pay fines or even go to jail for their beliefs. Among them were members of the Fitzherbert family.

Bishop Robert Pursglove was born in the Peak District village of Tideswell in 1504. By the time Henry VIII dissolved England's monasteries, he was prior of

Guisborough in Yorkshire. It fell to Pursglove to surrender the priory to the king in return for a pension. Henry VIII made him the Bishop of Hull, a post that he kept until the year after Elizabeth became queen. He was deprived of his office when he also refused to take the oath. He returned to Derbyshire, where he applied to the queen for letters patent to found a grammar school in Tideswell. It was called a grammar school because it taught Latin grammar to its pupils. When he died on 2 May 1579, he was buried in Tideswell Church. His brass shows him as a bishop dressed in robes worn during the reign of Mary but banned by Elizabeth.

DERBYSHIRE'S GRAMMAR SCHOOLS

Pursglove's was not the only grammar school to be founded during the Tudor period. Thomas Fanshawe from Holmesfield Gate Hall in the north of Derbyshire, Member of Parliament and the queen's rembrancer, whose duty it was to remind the Exchequer that taxes and records should be to the benefit of the Crown, founded a grammar school in Dronfield, carried out according to the wishes of his uncle, Henry Fanshawe, who left money in his will for the school. Both the Fanshawes and Pursglove were building on existing medieval traditions.

In 1559, a new grammar school at Repton was founded for scholars according to the terms of Sir John Port's will. His executors purchased the grounds of Repton Priory and its ruins for £37 10s and incorporated what remained into the new school there. In 1585, Ashbourne Grammar School received its royal charter from Queen Elizabeth I for incorporation. Like the other schools in Derbyshire, it was supported by a prominent member of the local gentry, Sir Thomas Cokayne, and was founded with the aim of providing a basic education for poor children.

A Derbyshire Romance

Sir George Vernon of Haddon Hall was the last of his line. His heirs were his daughters Margaret and Dorothy. A legend grew at the beginning of the nineteenth century that George disliked Dorothy's suitor, Sir John Manners, who was a younger son, so the pair eloped in 1563, during the wedding celebrations following Margaret's marriage to one of the Earl of Derby's sons. The story led to the publication of two novels, a play and a film about the couple that cemented the tale in the popular imagination.

Sir John, a son of the Earl of Rutland, was an eligible match, and even if the couple did run away, they were soon reconciled to Vernon. Dorothy inherited Haddon Hall, which remains the property of the Manners family to this day. Dorothy and her husband are buried in the Vernon family chapel at Bakewell.

Bess of Hardwick

Elizabeth Hardwick was not an heiress when she was born in 1527 at the house now known as Hardwick Old Hall. Her family were a part of Derbyshire's minor gentry. She made her first marriage, when she was 12 years old, to Robert Barlow, the son of one of her neighbours. He died the following year, and in 1547 she married Sir William Cavendish, by whom she had her six children.

After Cavendish's death in 1557, Bess married Sir William St Lowe, captain of Elizabeth I's guard. Widowed for a third time in 1567, she made her final marriage to George Talbot, 6th Earl of Shrewsbury, whose main residence was at Sheffield Castle. Bess had become one of the richest women in the country by the time of her wedding to Talbot. Her rise to wealth and power was reflected by the magnificent houses that she built during her lifetime.

Bess's earliest building project at Chatsworth does not survive. It was incorporated into the 1st Duke of Devonshire's palatial residence during the eighteenth century. In 1590, the countess redeveloped her childhood home, known as Old Hall, and then began work on a new mansion inspired by the Italian renaissance at Hardwick. She commissioned architect Robert Smythson to design her new home, which was built a short distance from the house where she was born. Completed in 1597, the resulting building, with its rooftop balustrades incorporating Bess's initials as an E.S. motif, is one of the finest examples of Elizabethan architecture in the country. Its vast array of windows, installed at a time when glass was extremely expensive, lead to the rhyme 'Hardwick Hall, more glass than wall.'

MARY QUEEN OF SCOTS IN DERBYSHIRE

Mary Queen of Scots fled to England in May 1568, and was committed into the care of the Earl and Countess of Shrewsbury in 1569 with instructions to keep her secure.

She was taken first to Walton Hall near Chesterfield, before being transferred to Wingfield Manor near Alfreton. She spent most of the next fourteen years in captivity at Sheffield Castle, but on occasion she was moved between Wingfield Manor, Bolsover and Chatsworth in Derbyshire.

Initially Bess of Hardwick and the Scottish queen formed a friendship based, in part, on their shared interest in embroidery, but relations soon became embittered because of Mary's complaints; the amount of time that the Earl of Shrewsbury spent in the queen's company; and Bess's own ambitions, which included arranging the marriage of her own daughter, Elizabeth Cavendish, to Mary's brother-in-law Charles Stuart, 5th Earl of Lennox.

During her time in his custody, Shrewsbury arranged for the Scottish queen to visit Buxton on five different occasions to take the waters, in the hope that it would cure her various ailments. As well as headaches, she was crippled by arthritis. The earl built New Hall, currently New Hall Hotel, Buxton, in 1572 so that the queen and the earl's own guests could access the spa waters at St Anne's Well. It soon became a popular location for courtiers from London to visit. Robert Dudley, Earl of Leicester, Queen Elizabeth's favourite, made several trips to the Peak District. Mary made her last visit in July 1584 and left a message written in glass with a diamond ring.

In November 1584, Shrewsbury was relieved of his role of gaoler and replaced by Ralph Sadler, who gave orders for his prisoner to be moved to Tutbury in Staffordshire. By then Shrewsbury's marriage to Bess was in tatters because of her ambitions and extravagant building projects. His health was broken and any hope of political power he might once have nursed were at an end.

THE BABINGTON PLOT

Many Catholics saw the Scottish queen as England's rightful monarch. This led to plots to release Mary from captivity and assassinate Elizabeth. Among the men who plotted Elizabeth's death was Anthony Babington of Dethick. In 1586, the young man was drawn into a conspiracy by Thomas Morgan, who worked for Mary's official agent in Paris, together with John Ballad, a Catholic priest. The plan was for the Spanish to provide financial backing for a French invasion of England. Queen Elizabeth was to be assassinated, allowing Mary to take her place on the throne, restoring Catholicism to England.

Babington began a secret correspondence, written in code, with the queen. Unknown to the plotters, Sir Francis Walsingham, Elizabeth's principal secretary, was aware of the conspiracy and employed Thomas Phelippes to break the cipher. On 17 July 1586, Mary wrote to Babington affirming her desire for freedom. She did not forbid the murder of Elizabeth. The Bond of Association devised in 1584, and signed by the Scottish queen, clearly stated that not only were conspirators of treason plots to be executed, but so was anyone in whose interest the plot was made. When he wrote his translation of the letter, Phelippes drew gallows on it because she was entrapped by her own words. The failed plot was the catalyst for Mary's execution at Fotheringhay on 8 February 1587, as well as Babington's own execution by hanging, drawing and quartering.

THE PADLEY MARTYRS

Many landed Derbyshire families clung to their religious beliefs. The Babingtons, Eyres and Fitzherberts, all related by marriage, were noted Catholics. The Eyre family came from Normandy to Derbyshire with William the Conqueror in 1066. Throughout the medieval period they held administrative roles, including warden of the forests of Edale, Hassop and Derwent. Now, in Tudor times, they were not permitted to become doctors or lawyers; they could not be executors of a will or become the guardians of a minor; nor could they travel more than 5 miles from home without a licence.

Sir John Fitzherbert of Padley Hall a fourteenth-century manor house near Hathersage, was discovered on 12 July 1588, the year of the Spanish Armada, by the Earl of Shrewsbury to be sheltering two Catholic priests, Robert Ludlam and Nicholas Garlick. The former was the son of a farmer from Radbourne and the latter was the son of a yeoman from Glossop. Fitzherbert, ten servants and the two priests were taken first to Sheffield before being moved to Derby for trial. On 23 July, the priests were charged with treason and Fitzherbert was indicted with sheltering them.

The two priests were hanged, drawn and quartered on St Mary's Bridge, Derby, the following day, along with a third priest named Richard Simpson who had been condemned before Easter. Their shattered remains were displayed as a warning to others. Today there is a plaque on the bridge recording their fate.

Sir John remained in Derby jail for the next two years but was eventually transported to London, where he died in 1591. His home fell into disrepair. All that remains today of Padley Hall is the gatehouse that was restored, in 1933, as a chapel to the two priests. A pilgrimage to the chapel takes place in July every year, where a special service is held in memory of the martyrs who were recognised as saints by Pope John Paul II in 1987.

DERBYSHIRE'S WITCHES

The Tudor and Stuart periods were a time when people feared witches. People who lived near caves and caverns in Derbyshire were concerned that these were the entrances to Hell. They gouged witchmarks in the walls and at entranceways to ward off evil spirits. The symbols were thought to turn away witches and demons and prevent them from crossing any threshold on which they were found. Examples can be found at Poole's Cavern near Buxton, as well as at Treak Cliff Cavern at Castleton. Hundreds more are carved into the walls and ceilings of Creswell Crags caves, guarding against whatever was lurking in the darkness. Some of the witch-marks look like daisies with six semicircular petals. Others look like an inverted letter W. The symbol is made from two Vs on top of one another, calling on the protection of Mary, mother of Christ; the letters stand for 'Virgin of Virgins'. Other protective marks include tear-shaped taper burns in beams and lintels.

In 1586, John Darrell, a preacher from Mansfield in Nottinghamshire, claimed that he exorcised a demon from the body of Katherine Wright of Eckington by the power of his prayers. Katherine accused her neighbour Margaret Roper of being the witch responsible for her bedevilment. Margaret was tried for witchcraft but the local justice, Sir Godfrey Foljambe, cleared her and accused Darrell of wasting the court's time.

Ten years later, in 1596, Alice Gooderidge was held in Derby gaol, where witchcraft charges were levelled against her by a 14-year-old boy called Thomas Darling. He claimed she caused him to be possessed by a demon after he encountered her in Winsell Wood near Stapenhill, which is now in Staffordshire. When Alice proved unable to recite the Lord's Prayer, Sir Humphrey Ferrers and a local magistrate, Thomas Gresley, instructed that Alice, and her elderly mother Elizabeth Wright, should be searched for witchmarks where the devil or a witch's familiar were said to suck blood. Elizabeth was stripped and searched for blemishes, which were soon found. Alice, desperate to avoid the charge of witchcraft, cut a wart from her belly leaving a gaping wound. The next step in the interrogation was to 'warm' Alice's feet over an open fire. Unsurprisingly, Alice confessed. The Witchcraft Act of 1563 stipulated that rather than execution, Alice, as a first-time offender, should be sent to prison for a year. In 1599, after Alice's death, Darling confirmed that he invented the story, but by then a pamphlet entitled *The most wonderfull and true storie of a certin witch, Alice Gooderidge of Stepenhill* was doing the rounds.

5

STUART DERBYSHIRE: A CIVIL WAR

In 1610, John Speed, the mapmaker, visited Derbyshire. His atlas, *The Theatre of the Empire of Great Britaine*, was published in 1611 and 1612. The map of Derbyshire, speckled with hills, included a plan of Derby and Buxton, whose waters remained popular. All Saints Church remained at the heart of Derby. Little had changed since 1200. The timber-framed buildings still sat on the long narrow burgage plots established in the medieval period, but there were an increasing number of stone-built houses. Derbyshire's gentry wanted town houses as well as their country manors. Many of them were becoming much wealthier because of the mineral wealth of their land and their increasing involvement in industry. The Cavendish and Manners families' lead-mining interests supplied half of Europe's needs by the beginning of the seventeenth century.

In the countryside, hollow ways continued to be used as a transport network, but there were more packhorses than ever before moving goods and materials across the county. Roads were virtually impossible for heavy wagons throughout the winter months. New packhorse bridges, such as the one in the Goyt valley and at Holme Bridge, Bakewell, were built across rivers and streams so that ponies and their panniers could cross safely. The bridges, arched for strength and to allow for swollen waters, were wide enough to let one animal cross at a time, and low parapets permitted the clearance of panniers slung on each side of the animal. Between 1650 and 1800, long strings of packhorses carried all manner of goods across the county, including salt, lead, iron ore, coal and corn. Ryknield Street continued to be the most important north-south route for transport but lead, iron ore and coal was increasingly shipped by barge along the Trent to the Humber estuary and on to the port of Hull.

Arbella Stuart

Plots against the Crown continued even after James VI of Scotland ascended the throne as James I of England in 1603. Bess of Hardwick's granddaughter, Arbella, was a focus for some of the conspiracies that surrounded the throne. She inherited royal Tudor blood from her father, Charles Stewart, Earl of Lennox. His family were descended from Margaret Tudor's second marriage to Archibald Douglas, 6th Earl of Angus. Arbella, the daughter of Elizabeth Cavendish, was born on 10 November 1575. Charles died within five months of her birth. Before James became king, Arbella was carefully guarded by her grandmother at Hardwick Hall. It was an isolated and unhappy existence. When James became king of England, Arbella's fortunes improved, as did those of her relations. In 1605, her uncle, William Cavendish, who purchased Chatsworth from his elder brother Henry, became the 1st Earl of Devonshire.

James invited Arbella, who was fourth in line to the throne, to live at court, where he treated her with kindness. By 1608, the king, who was in no hurry to see his cousin married, promised that she could wed who she wished so long as her chosen husband was neither a foreigner nor a Catholic. William Seymour, the grandson of 1st Earl of Hertford and Katherine Grey, the sister of Lady Jane Grey, proposed to Arbella and she accepted. The king was furious. The couple were both descended from the Tudors. Their union presented a threat to the security of his own crown. Seymour was hauled before the royal council and publicly retracted his promise of marriage.

The pair planned to run away together, having married in secret with Arbella's steward, Hugh Compton, as a witness. On 8 July 1610, when the king was informed, he ordered that William and Arbella should be arrested. William was sent to the Tower while Arbella, who feigned illness, was placed in the care of Sir Thomas Parry at his home in Lambeth. The king became increasingly suspicious and sent his own doctor to examine her. James ordered that she be sent north, but Arbella became so hysterical that she travelled no further than Barnet.

While Arbella was in Barnet, her Aunt Mary, Countess of Shrewsbury, who was Bess of Hardwick's eldest daughter, set in motion a plan to help the couple escape. Arbella persuaded her guard to allow her to visit the Tower to say a final farewell to William and then, disguised as a man, boarded a French boat bound for Calais. The ship was late departing because William was delayed. The vessel was intercepted just before it reached safety, and Arbella returned to London. She spent the last four years of her life in the Tower. The Countess of Shrewsbury was required to pay a fine of £20,000. William Seymour managed to escape to Holland, but was permitted to return to England in 1615 after Arbella's death.

WILLIAM CAVENDISH OF BOLSOVER

After Gilbert Talbot, 7th Earl of Shrewsbury's death in 1616, and that of his brother, Edward, in 1618, the Talbots' Derbyshire estates were divided between Gilbert and Mary Cavendish's three daughters: the Countesses of Pembroke, Arundel and Kent. Mary Talbot was unhappily married to William Herbert, 3rd Earl of Pembroke, who took possession of Chesterfield, the hundred of Scarsdale and Wingfield Manor. In 1631, the earl sold much of the inheritance to his wife's cousin, William Cavendish, who, as the sole surviving male heir of Charles Cavendish, Bess of Hardwick's third son, inherited all his own father's estates.

William, who saw himself as a poet and playwright as well as a nobleman thanks to honours achieved through marriage and royal favour, renovated and extended Bolsover Castle. The medieval castle became a lavish pleasure palace for the fun-loving courtier, who even designed Italianate gardens of the kind he saw during a trip to Europe in his youth. Cavendish was also renowned as a breeder and trainer of horses. He used kinder techniques than many of his contemporaries at his stables and indoor riding school at Bolsover, and wrote a book on the subject.

King Charles I, who succeeded his father as king in 1625, visited Derbyshire on several occasions, staying with Cavendish, who became the Earl of Newcastle in 1628. In 1638, William was appointed governor to King Charles I's 8-year-old heir, Prince Charles, with instructions to teach him riding and swordsmanship.

Derbyshire, Charles I and the English Civil War

In 1625, Charles demanded a forced loan from his wealthier subjects because Parliament would not grant him the funds that he believed to be a royal prerogative. In Derbyshire, men, including the Earl of Devonshire, refused to supply the king's demands unless it was sanctioned by Parliament. Further taxes and forced loans were widely resented in Derbyshire. By 1628, Parliament raised objections to Charles's approach to government, and so, between 1629 and 1641, the king ruled without it.

Charles was not able to levy any new taxes because parliamentary approval was required. Instead, he used existing measures and older royal rights as a way of raising funds. In Derbyshire, lead mined on Crown or Duchy of Lancaster lands accrued a fee known as 'fother', stemming from the monarch's ancient claim to lead ore and to all the mineral rights in the area, known as the King's Field. Taxation on miners rose from 20s to 48s per fother, or 22½ hundredweight, of smelted lead.

Even worse was the demand for a tax known as 'ship money'. In 1635, Derbyshire's high sheriff was sent a ship money assessment of £3,500, of which the town of Derby was required to contribute £175. The tax was within the king's rights, but in medieval times it was levied only in coastal areas when the realm was at war. Charles extended the tax inland at a time when the country was at peace. Sir John Stanhope of Elvaston, whose elder half-brother Philip was Earl of Chesterfield, refused to pay a penny. His goods were seized and he was sent to London under arrest.

DERBYSHIRE GOES TO WAR

Charles passed through Derby in 1642 on his way to Nottingham, where he raised the royal standard marking the start of England's civil war. In all about twenty men from Derby followed the king to enter his service. William Cavendish, the Earl of Newcastle, became the Royalist commander of Derbyshire's militia. He remained staunchly Royalist throughout the civil war, becoming general of the king's forces north of the River Trent, but the rest of the county was predominantly Parliamentarian in its sympathies.

Sir John Gell of Hopton Hall, near Wirksworth, descended from a family who became rich and powerful from lead mining, raised a regiment for Parliament even though the king had created him a baronet in January 1642. He obtained a commission as colonel from the Earl of Essex to secure Derbyshire against the king. His decision was based, in part, on the fact that the Stanhope family supported the Crown.

Gell commandeered Derby's town hall on 31 October and fortified Derby against Royalist forces. He ensured that there was a man permanently on lookout at the top of All Saints Church tower for fear that Royalists might attack.

As governor of Derby, a post he held for the next four years, Gell was able to conscript men to build the town's earthwork defences, as well as a gunpowder mill.

During the first winter of the civil war, word reached Gell that a Royalist contingent was fortifying Swarkestone Bridge, 8 miles to the south of Derby. On 5 January 1643, he struck the works and drove the Royalists off, and was able to hold the strategic north–south crossing for the whole of the war, unlike the bridges at Burton and Nottingham, which changed hands several times. Afterwards he took his men to Lichfield, where his enemy, the Earl of Chesterfield, had taken control of the town. When the earl surrendered in March, Gell sent him to London in chains.

Gell's next engagement with Royalist forces was at Hopton Heath in Staffordshire on 19 March 1643. The Royalist commander, Spencer Compton, 2nd Earl of Northampton, was killed by the Parliamentarians when he was unhorsed and separated from his troops, but Gell was forced to withdraw to Derby when the Royalists captured most of his artillery. By then Parliamentarian troops had run out of bullets and were clubbing their enemies to death with their weapons. Gell took the body of Northampton with him. He offered to return Compton's remains in exchange for artillery captured from the Parliamentarians and repayment for the cost of embalming Northampton's body. When the new earl refused Gell's terms, he had the naked corpse dragged around the town before consigning it to the Cavendish vault in All Saints Church.

In April 1643, the Earl of Newcastle garrisoned Bolsover Castle, the only remaining Royalist stronghold in the county, but it was the end of the year before he began his own campaign. Six country houses in the north of the county were garrisoned by Parliamentary forces, including Chatsworth, Sutton Scarsdale Hall and Staveley, which had been taken from the Royalists. In December he advanced upon Chesterfield, and, having captured it, the earl moved on Wingfield Manor, where Mary Queen of Scots had once been imprisoned. At the outbreak of the civil war the 4th Earl of Pembroke, who owned it, garrisoned the manor for Parliament. The Earl of Newcastle intended to take it for the king even though it was surrounded by strong defences. On 19 December, after a twelve-day siege, the Parliamentarians decided to accept Newcastle's offer to allow them to leave.

Newcastle gave orders to add a huge earthen embankment to the defences and left Colonel Dalby in charge. The earl pushed into the Peak District through Bakewell towards Hartington. Had Newcastle advanced on Derby it is likely that he would have won the county for the king's cause, but in January 1644 a Scottish army crossed the Tweed in support of Parliament. Cavendish had no option but to abandon his campaign in Derbyshire.

Newcastle departed for Yorkshire, taking 2,300 Derbyshire recruits with him. It was not long before Gell forced the withdrawal of Royalists from Ashbourne, Bakewell and Tissington. He turned his attention to the garrison at Wingfield, placing the manor under siege once again, but it proved even harder to breach the defences than it had before. In Yorkshire, on 2 July 1644, cavalrymen from Derbyshire under the command of Rowland Eyre took their place in the left wing of the Royalist army at Marston Moor. After three hours of fighting the king's army was defeated, and most of the men who survived the battle retreated to York. The Earl of Newcastle fled the country, taking no further part in the civil war. One consequence of the battle was that the garrison at Wingfield was at the mercy of Gell's Parliamentarian artillery.

Eyre led the remnants of his force back to Derbyshire, where they were ordered to aid the men at Wingfield. Eyre's own brother, Thomas, was among their number. The cavaliers rested overnight at Boylestone Church, in the Derbyshire Dales. A Parliamentarian force captured the whole contingent of 200 men while they slept. Their removal meant that the garrison at Wingfield could expect no help. The Royalists refused to surrender to Gell's men, but on 14 August 1644 Parliamentarian artillery breached the walls and retook Wingfield after a siege that lasted ten weeks.

On 14 June 1645, Gell and his men failed to arrive in time to take part in the Battle of Naseby in Northamptonshire. King Charles advanced into Derbyshire in August 1645, skirmishing with Parliamentarians at Sudbury and Ashbourne. He rested overnight at Ashbourne Hall before marching through Derbyshire to Doncaster.

Derbyshire was in the hands of Parliament. Sir George Gresley of Drakelow described a county ravaged by both armies; of halls and manors captured first by one side and then the other; of horses requisitioned and the demand that Parliamentarian soldiers be provided with free lodging. Sir John Gell offered administrative posts to his friends and relatives and allowed his men to plunder as they wished.

Gell, whose reputation was tarnished by his failure to join General Fairfax at Naseby, was summoned to London to answer to a Parliamentary Committee. His men were incorporated into the New Model Army on the orders of Oliver Cromwell. Sir Thomas Fairfax came to Derby to ensure that the garrison complied with the orders, and stripped Gell of his governorship of the town. In June 1646, the fortifications at Derby and Wingfield were removed by order of Parliament.

In 1648, by which time King Charles was a prisoner in Carisbrooke Castle on the Isle of Wight, there were a series of Royalist uprisings. In July, a Scottish army crossed the border in support of the king. On 18 August, they were routed by Cromwell at Preston in Lancashire. Defeated soldiers scattered across Derbyshire in the hope that they might be able to hide themselves. On 14 September, 1,500 fleeing Scottish infantrymen were rounded up and imprisoned in the church at Chapel-en-le-Frith. Forty-four men died from starvation or their injuries in the sixteen days they remained there. The parish register records their burials.

COMMONWEALTH DERBYSHIRE

King Charles I was executed on 30 January 1649. The Royalist families in the county paid a heavy price for their loyalty to the crown. Philip Stanhope, 1st Earl of Chesterfield, who had been in the Tower since the surrender of Lichfield to the Parliamentarian army in 1643, forfeited his possessions. He died in 1656, still a prisoner of the state, mourning the loss of two sons during the civil war. The Earl of Newcastle was in exile in Holland. Parliament declared him to be a traitor and seized his estates. It left him and his new wife, Margaret, facing an uncertain financial future. In

Derbyshire, Bolsover Castle was to be sold and made untenable. Its new owners began to demolish it and sell the stone. It was only saved because Newcastle's brother, Sir Charles Cavendish, who had already been forced to sell off much of his own land to pay the fine demanded by the Committee for the Compounding of Delinquents, sold more of his own property to buy back Bolsover.

The Earl of Devonshire, who took no part in the civil war, having departed for France at the start of the conflict to preserve his inheritance, paid a fine of £5,000 to avoid the charge of delinquency and returned to live quietly with his mother in Buckinghamshire. Chatsworth was damaged by its use as a garrison, first by one side and then the other. The Earl of Devonshire's younger brother, Colonel Charles Cavendish, who financed a regiment with the earl's money, was killed at the Battle of Gainsborough in Lincolnshire in 1643.

Cromwell died in September 1658. The following year, Philip Stanhope, 2nd Earl of Chesterfield since his grandfather's death in 1656, became involved with a Royalist plot known as Booth's Rising. He and other Royalists attacked Parliamentary militia in Nottinghamshire but were forced to retreat. One of their leaders, Colonel Charles White, fled to Derby, where Charles II was declared king in the marketplace during the morning of 12 August. The town was back in the hands of Parliament that afternoon and Booth's Rising collapsed a week later. Stanhope was briefly imprisoned in the Tower before travelling to the Royalist court in Holland.

LEVIATHAN

King Charles II was restored to his throne on 25 May 1660. The Earl of Devonshire returned to Chatsworth. He was appointed Lord Lieutenant of Derbyshire as well as Steward of the High Peak.

He was joined by his old tutor, the philosopher Thomas Hobbes, who was also, briefly, Charles II's teacher. Hobbes was best known for his book *Leviathan* that compared the state to a monster and explored whether or not a subject had the right to rebel against a weak ruler. Without a strong central authority, Hobbes believed, life would be nasty, brutish and short. He also wrote, in 1636, a poem about Derbyshire that described seven 'wonders' and which was, in effect, the first guide to the Peak District. Poole's Cavern, Mam Tor and the well that ebbed and flowed at Tideswell were on his list, as was Chatsworth.

Prior to the civil war, Hobbes lived at Hardwick Hall and was responsible for its library. He returned there with the earl and remained there for the rest of his life, dying aged 91 years, in December 1679. He was buried at Ault Hucknall Church, where his memorial recorded his long life.

PLAGUE

In 1665, Derby was deserted as bubonic plague took hold. Grass began to grow where the market was usually held because farmers refused to enter the town. Instead, the townspeople left money in exchange for goods at the 'Headless Cross' at Friar Gate leading from Derby in the direction of Ashbourne. The 1791 *History of Derby* written by William Hutton explained that a container of vinegar was used to disinfect the coin that paid for the goods, which were purchased at arm's length.

During the late summer of 1665, a carter arrived at the village of Eyam in the Peak District. He was carrying a parcel of cloth for Alexander Hadfield, the tailor. The cloth was damp from its journey, so the tailor's assistant, George Viccars, hung it by the fire to dry. By September Viccars was dead and plague was spreading rapidly among the people of Eyam.

The infection continued to spread throughout the autumn, killing forty-two men, women and children, but appeared to be on the wane during the winter months. During the spring of 1666, the plague returned with more force. People began to discuss the possibility of going to stay with family and friends to escape the disease.

Fearful of what might happen if the plague arrived in nearby Bakewell or Sheffield, Reverend William Mompesson began his campaign to persuade the people of Eyam not to leave. He sent for the Reverend Thomas Stanley, who had been dismissed as Eyam's vicar in April 1664 when he refused to use the Book of Common Prayer introduced in 1662. Stanley, like many of the men and women in Eyam, was a puritan and much more popular with the villagers than Mompesson. Together the two men made a plan and contacted the Earl of Devonshire, who agreed to send the village necessary food and supplies while they remained in quarantine.

The villagers agreed in August not to flee. Instead, they would try to contain the disease within the parish's boundaries. As the summer heat intensified, the death toll began to

rise once more. Elizabeth Hancock buried her husband and six of her children in just eight days in a field next to the family farm. It had been agreed that people would bury their own dead close to the homes where they died rather than taking the bodies to the churchyard. A man named Marshall Howe, who survived the plague, acted as grave digger and under-taker when entire families were wiped out. Among the dead were his own wife and son. Mompesson's wife, Catherine, died on the morning of 22 August 1666. Hers would be the only burial in the churchyard that summer. From a popula-tion of approximately 800 people, 260 died. On 1 November 1666, Abraham Morten became the last person to die from the plague in Eyam.

THE GLORIOUS REVOLUTION

King Charles II died in 1685. His brother, the Duke of York, became James II with widespread support. This was despite the fact that some MPs, including Derby's representative Robert Coke, wanted James excluded from the succession because of his Catholic beliefs. It did not help that the new king favoured absolute monarchy without any limits imposed on what he might do. The majority of Derbyshire's gentry belonged to the Tory party, who objected to King James's desire for religious freedoms for Catholics, but argued that a stable society was founded on a system based on birthright. No one wanted another civil war. Besides which, James's heir was his eldest daughter Mary, from James's first marriage to Ann Hyde. Mary and her husband, William of Orange, the Stadtholder of Holland, were both Protestants.

In 1688, tensions between King James II and his people intensified when the king granted freedom of worship to Catholics and non-conformists alike. It was seen as an attack on the Church of England. Even worse, the king's second wife, Mary of Modena, gave birth to a baby boy named James after his father on 10 June. The arrival of a male heir established a Catholic Stuart dynasty. Soon a rumour swept taverns that the infant was a changeling smuggled into the palace in a warming pan.

William Cavendish, 4th Earl of Devonshire, was one of the leaders of the Whig Party that opposed the idea of absolute monarchy and granting rights to Catholics. In August 1688, Devonshire, the Earl of Danby, and John D'Arcy, Lord Conyers, a younger son of the Earl of Holderness, met at the Cock and Pynot Inn at Old Whittington near Chesterfield, now called Revolution House. They claimed to be a hunting party seeking shelter from the rain. In reality the three noblemen were plotting how they might depose the king.

The Earl of Devonshire became one of the so-called 'immortal seven' who signed an invitation to William of Orange and Mary inviting them to invade England. William arrived in England on 5 November 1688 at Torbay in Devon. The original plan was for the earl to seize Nottingham, but when news arrived of the successful landing at Torbay, he claimed Derby for the prince. On 23 December, King James went into exile, and in April 1689, William and Mary became joint monarchs. In May, the earl was appointed Lord Lieutenant of Derbyshire. He was also made a privy councillor and Lord Steward of the Royal Household. In 1694, he was created Marquis of Hartington and 1st Duke of Devonshire.

The duke found time to renovate Chatsworth House, which had fallen into disrepair across the years. He added a magnificent State Apartment, the Painted Hall and a long gallery, as well as remodelling the exterior. Chatsworth was finished in 1707, not that William had long to enjoy it before his own death. The new duke, another William, followed his father into the Whig Party and played a prominent part in the government of King George I. The 3rd Duke followed the same career path as his father and grandfather. Each generation made lucrative marriages that brought new estates and wealth into the family, allowing them to extend Chatsworth, its park and gardens, as well as to invest in works of art. The 4th Duke, who was prime minister for a short time, even moved the village of Edensor to improve the view from Chatsworth.

DERBYSHIRE'S SEVENTEENTH-CENTURY BUILDING CRAZE

In 1663, Philip Kinder produced a history of the county. It was a period of growing prosperity for landowners, who were quick to benefit from the mineral resources on their land. Coal mining had become one of the county's principal industries. Lead remained profitable and the iron industry was developing rapidly. Other industries, including glass, brick-making and pottery manufacture, also thrived.

Wealth generated by trade and industry was reflected in the building works of the period. At the start of the century, in 1609, Tissington Hall was built by Sir Francis FitzHerbert to replace the medieval dwelling on the same site. Renishaw Hall near Chesterfield was built in about 1625 by the ironmaster George Sitwell. The family owned furnaces at Foxbrooke, near Renishaw, and at South Wingfield. The industry relied on wood to make the charcoal that was needed to power the furnaces. Dwindling wood supplies limited the amount of pig iron that could be created within the county. Sudbury Hall, south of Ashbourne, with its baroque exterior, was started by George Vernon in 1665. At Calke, Sir John Harpur began work incorporating the old priory and Tudor house into the present building as the Stuart period came to its end.

A little closer to Derby, Melbourne, which had its roots as a medieval deer park and bishop's palace, was in the hands of the Coke family. Sir John Coke, who purchased the house in 1629, was Charles I's Secretary of State. He demolished the remains of the medieval building and built an Elizabethan-style manor. The Coke family suffered at the hands of Parliament during the English Civil War and had to buy back the estate, which had been confiscated when Charles II was restored to the throne. By 1699, Thomas Coke was planning to create gardens at Melbourne in a similar style to those popularised by King Louis XIV at Versailles. Coke would continue to enhance the gardens at Melbourne with a yew tunnel, a specially built grotto, statues, and even a wrought-iron arbour created for him by master ironsmith Robert Bakewell in 1706.

6

GEORGIAN DERBYSHIRE: REVOLUTIONS AND REBELLIONS

Derbyshire was changing from an agricultural to an industrial economy, and with it came the demand for better transport networks. The answer was the establishment of turnpike roads run by trusts created by parliamentary acts. These routes shifted the cost of road maintenance from individual parishes to the people who used the roads. The trustees used loans to fund the road building and used tollgates or tollbars, with a keeper's cottage, where fees for using the road were collected to pay off the loan. Mail coaches were exempted from tolls. Instead, their guards sounded their horns as the coach approached and the keeper opened the tollgate to let

the mail through. New roads were built on less steep gradients, connecting Derby to Leek, Macclesfield and Manchester. Turnpike trusts were also established to improve the journey from Derbyshire to Sheffield and to Nottingham. Even so, at Grindleford, coach passengers travelling from Buxton to Sheffield were often asked to get out and walk up the hill so that the horses could pull the coach to the top.

ALL SAINTS CHURCH, DERBY

By 1713, All Saints was in a serious state of disrepair. The main body of the church and the roof had become so ruinous that they were a danger to the congregation. In 1714, Derby received a Letter Patent from the Crown permitting a collection, which raised £500, to help pay for an extensive building programme.

An argument began about whether the existing church should be repaired or whether it should be completely demolished and replaced by a new building. The minister of All Saints, Dr Michael Hutchinson, wanted to start afresh, but was opposed by the Derby Corporation and by parishioners who loved their medieval church. The argument raged back and forth for the next nine years, during which time St Mary's continued to decay. In February 1723, Hutchinson issued orders for a team of workmen to demolish parts of the church overnight. The Corporation, who were still arguing about the best way forward, had no option other than to rebuild.

Hutchinson selected a plan by the architect James Gibbs, who designed St Martin-in-the-Fields Church in London. The new church retained its sixteenth-century 65m-tall tower and medieval porch but the rest of it was rebuilt according to neoclassical principles. The new fittings included a wrought-iron chancel screen made by the celebrated ironsmith Robert Bakewell. The church was complete by November 1725 and the screen was installed five years later.

DERBY'S SILK SPY

Daniel Defoe visited Derby during his travels in 1725. He described it as a prosperous cloth town. However, the silk that the mills produced was much inferior to the twisted silk thread produced in the Piedmont region of Italy. Thomas Lombe, a mill owner, financed his half-brother John's visit there in 1714. His task was to find out how the Italians made silk thread strong enough to use as the warp for weaving silk fabrics. John found a job in one of Piedmont's factories, where he discovered the secret lay in the silk throwing machines that twisted the threads before winding them onto bobbins for spinning. He smuggled plans back to England in bales of silk before returning home.

In 1718, Thomas Lombe obtained patents for winding, spinning and twisting silk into organzine, made of several silk threads twisted together, and then twisted again in the opposite direction to the original yarn. He invested in a five-storey silk mill on the River Derwent, as well as the machinery that would wind, spin and twist raw silk thread ready to be woven or knitted into cloth. John died unexpectedly on 16 March 1722. It was said that he was poisoned by an Italian woman sent to wreak vengeance on the man whose espionage had ruined Piedmont's silk monopoly.

'A HOWLING WILDERNESS' AND ITS LEAD MINERS

When Daniel Defoe visited the Peak District, he described the region as a 'howling wilderness'. Defoe spoke with a lead miner who explained that the shaft he worked was 360ft deep. He envied men who were able to emerge from a hole in the side of a hill rather than make the dangerous ascent up the side of a wood-lined shaft.

Miners used hammers, picks and wedges to split the rock. Once their baskets or 'wiskets' were full, they placed them on sledges known as 'corves', which they dragged back to the bottom of the shaft. Windlasses were then used to lift the wiskets to the surface. By the 1660s gunpowder was being used to blast shafts, and if the lead veins were located in rock that was difficult to dig, they sometimes built fires against the rockface and allowed them to burn through the night. The following morning the miners threw water on the heated rock to help it to splinter. It required the skills of an experienced fire setter if accidents were to be avoided. While men worked down the mine, women did much of the work on the surface, removing more of the rock from the ore, or dressing it, before it was sold.

BONNIE PRINCE CHARLIE IN DERBY

When King James II fled England in 1688, he did not give up hope of reclaiming his kingdom. Upon his death in 1701, he was succeeded by his son, who was known to his supporters as King James III and to his opponents as 'the Pretender'. His eldest son, Charles Edward Stuart, Bonnie Prince Charlie, led a major Jacobite rebellion in 1745. Initial success in Scotland against the Hanoverian army of King George III, in September 1745, was followed, that autumn, by Bonnie Prince Charlie marching south at the head of an army.

In Derbyshire, the Reverend James Clegg of Chapel-en-le-Frith recorded the growing panic of his neighbours as the Jacobite army advanced. On 27 September, the Duke of Devonshire, the Lord Lieutenant of the county, summoned the local gentry to meet at Derby to discuss how they might raise a force for the defence of the realm. He opted to raise a militia paid for by public donation. He named the regiment the Derbyshire Blues. Its officers were commissioned by King George. At the end of November, the duke reviewed 700 men in Derby. Half of them were led by Sir Nathaniel Curzon of Kedleston Hall, while the rest were commanded by the duke's own eldest son, the Marquis of Hartington.

On 3 December, intelligence arrived in Derby that the Jacobites, having advanced from Manchester to Macclesfield and from there to Leek, skirting the Peak District, were in Ashbourne. The Derbyshire Blues promptly withdrew to Retford near Nottingham, where they regrouped. Their officers had no desire to confront an army that was rumoured to be 9,000 strong.

At exactly 11 o'clock on 4 December, two mounted soldiers advanced along Friar Gate in the direction of Derby's town hall and occupied the George Inn, which had recently been the duke's headquarters. Soon afterwards, an army of footsore soldiers and clansmen arrived to the skirl of bagpipes. The Jacobites captured Derby without any opposition and proclaimed King James III in the marketplace. The *Derby Mercury*, which began publication in 1732, was uncomplimentary about the prince's followers, describing them as 'a parcel of shabby, lousy, pitiful looking fellows'. Even so, after capturing Carlisle on 18 November they were now only 125 miles from London, which was said to be in a state of panic. The prince sent a party to secure Swarkestone Bridge, about 6 miles south of Derby.

On Thursday, 5 December, after celebrating a Catholic Mass at All Saints Church, the prince's advisers met to decide their strategy. The first thing the council did was to exact the taxes owing to the Crown and then to demand that subscribers to the Derbyshire militia pay the same amount again into the prince's war chest. The prince had already visited a number of known supporters of the Stuart kings on his way to Derby, to raise funds to pay his men and supply them. Squire Meynell of Bradley Hall, a known Jacobite, received a visit, and although he had dined with the prince, the squire had taken the precaution of burying his silver in the garden beforehand. Men who drank to 'the king over the water' had little appetite for civil conflict on their own doorstep.

The prince's advisers were concerned that support from English Jacobites had failed to materialise and that hoped-for French support had not arrived. Charles's generals were alarmed that they might be trapped by government forces. As they argued about their next move, Eliezer Birch, an English spy, was captured and revealed that the road to London was blocked by forces loyal to the Hanoverian throne. Dudley Bradstreet, another government spy, met with the Duke of Cumberland, the king's young brother recalled from Europe's wars with his men to prevent a successful uprising, at Lichfield. Broadstreet continued his journey to Derby in the guise of a Jacobite. He informed the prince's council that there was a force of 9,000 men at Northampton. He convinced them that they were in danger of running into a government army poised to attack. They did not have sufficient intelligence of their own to know that it was a lie. The prince was reluctantly forced to agree that he and his army should return to Scotland.

'Black Friday' marked the start of the retreat led by Lord George Murray. The prince refused to lead a withdrawal that took the Jacobites back the way they had come. On 7 December, part of the prince's army passed back across the River Dove at Ashbourne and climbed the hill towards Mayfield. Villagers took refuge inside the church while soldiers took pot-shots at the west door, leaving bullet holes that can still be seen.

The fast-moving retreat from Derby damaged Prince Charles's relationship with his commanders, who led their men back into Scotland on 20 December 1745. The rising ended with the battle at Culloden on 16 April 1746, where hundreds of Jacobites were slaughtered.

INDUSTRIAL DERBYSHIRE

The Industrial Revolution saw Derbyshire's entrepreneurs, often from humble backgrounds, flourish when they were joined by men who were prepared to invest in their ideas. In 1756, Jedidiah Strutt, the son of a Derbyshire farmer, invented a knitting frame with turning needles that could produce either ribbed or unribbed cotton stockings. He patented the design in 1759. The technique was soon adapted to the production of other fabrics. In Derby, Strutt went into partnership with his brother-in-law, William Woollatt, who was a hosiery manufacturer. By the time Strutt's first patent, for the Derby Rib machine, expired he was a wealthy man.

Elsewhere in Derbyshire, Sir Richard Arkwright developed a water machine that permitted unskilled workers to spin ninety-six cotton threads at a time. He built the first water-powered cotton mill, at Cromford near Matlock, in 1771 using the principles employed by the Lombe silk mill at Derby. His enterprise was financed by Jedadiah Strutt, who paid £500 to join Arkwright in partnership with Samuel Need, a Nottingham hosier. Cromford Mill provided a successful model for other industrialists to copy.

In 1776, Strutt built his own cotton mill at Belper to harness the water power of the Derwent. More mills were built alongside the river as the century progressed. Arkwright's mill at Cromford expanded to include looms for turning cotton thread into calico as well as framework knitting. Strutt's three sons, William, George and Joseph, ran their father's factories between them after his death in 1797.

Both Strutt and Arkwright built factories and provided cottages for their workers that were regarded as being better than the average working person's accommodation. The Arkwright Houses at Cromford were the first he built. They included space on the second floor to allow their occupiers to work from home. He also built a church, chapel, school, shops and public houses. Cromford was a model settlement.

Peter Nightingale, a wealthy lead-smelting merchant, provided investment for Arkwright's mill and went on to build his own mill nearby at Lea in 1784. Lea Mills became the home of John Smedley Ltd, which is the oldest active mill as well as the oldest manufacturing business in the world. Nightingale also invested in the Cromford Canal Company and paid for the Lea Bridge arm of the canal network to connect his own mill to the system.

By 1789 there were twenty-two cotton spinning mills in Derbyshire and twelve silk mills in Derby, turning it into one of the most important silk-throwing towns in the country. Today, a 15-mile stretch of the River Derwent from Cromford through Belper to Derby carries World Heritage status. The Industrial Revolution changed Derbyshire and the rest of Britain for ever.

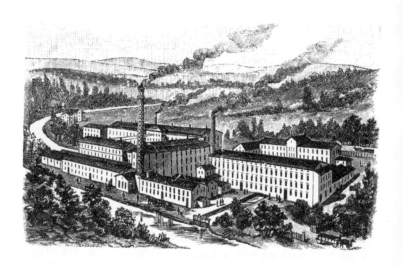

THE SCANDAL OF LITTON MILL

Ellis Needham and his cousin Thomas Frith built a cotton mill at Litton near Tideswell in 1782 on land leased from Lord Scarsdale, but the mill proved unprofitable and Frith left the company in 1799.

Because of the costs associated with labour, Needham decided to employ parish apprentices and flout the minimum standards established in 1802 for their care. The Poor Law Act of 1601 allowed churchwardens responsible for their parish's poor to come to an agreement with employers, by means of an indenture sworn before a Justice of the Peace that the employer would provide a job and training for the pauper child. At Litton this worked to the advantage of the employers, who used the children as cheap labour, keeping them in purpose-built apprentice houses, neglecting basic necessities and hygiene and feeding them 'porridge and black bread'. In return the children worked fourteen-hour days, six days a week, were beaten by brutal overseers and subject to frequent accidents with the machinery. Many of them died during their time in the mills. The need for the apprentices to be taught a skill or trade was also ignored.

Among their number was Robert Blincoe, an inmate of St Pancras Workhouse, London, indentured in 1799 with eighty other apprentices. As an adult, he wrote his memoirs and was an active campaigner for the abolition of child labour in England, giving his testimony to the Royal Commission on the Employment of Children. It is thought that Charles Dickens based the character of Oliver Twist on Blincoe's experiences.

AN AGE OF STEAM, COAL AND IRON

The growth of steam power saw a rising demand for coal, which had been extracted from Derbyshire's coal measures from Roman times onwards. By the eighteenth century, the mines were becoming ever deeper and more dangerous.

The coal measures contained beds of ironstone that had been used since the Norman invasion. There is a reference to a smith at Elvaston in the Domesday Book of 1085, and Derby's medieval market for iron goods was well known. All that remains today is a street named Irongate. Ironworkers were reliant on charcoal and water to manufacture iron, but by the sixteenth century wealthy landowners like the Earl of Shrewsbury were beginning to introduce blast furnaces to the industry. In 1642, coke was used to roast malt in Derbyshire, which improved the quality of the beer and enabled the production of pale ale. It was another fifty years before a coke-fired blast furnace to produce cast iron was developed and a method of producing coke from coal introduced. However, it was not until 1747 that a description of the new technology found its way into print and industrialists were able to build larger blast furnaces, bringing the price of cast iron down. The first coke furnace was built at Alderwasley, in the Amber Valley, in 1764. More coke furnaces were built near Heage. As the technology improved, the amount of pig iron produced by the county increased.

In 1774, John Smith of Chesterfield established the Griffin Foundry at Brampton, which included a furnace, boring mill and forge. The company expanded its capacity by using water wheels powered by the River Hipper at Furnace Hill. The firm produced cannon and cannon balls for the East India Company and for Wellington's army. It is said that the cannon balls fired at the Battle of Waterloo came from Smiths of Chesterfield. The firm continued to grow after the end of the Napoleonic Wars because it expanded its range of products to

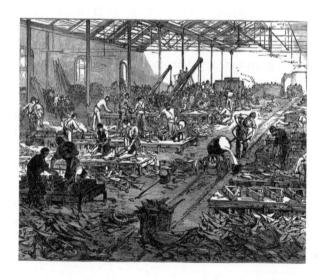

include the production of steam engines and pumping engines that powered the Industrial Revolution.

The Butterley Company was founded in 1790 by Benjamin Outram and Francis Beresford near Ripley. The company drew on Derbyshire's natural resources, including limestone from Crich as well as coal and iron ore. The following year it expanded as its owners took advantage of the growing demand for pig iron.

The skies were filled with fire, smoke and the sound of the rhythmic thump of hammers producing cast-iron goods that were used in Derbyshire and as far afield as India.

Its furnaces provided the ironwork for London's eleven-span Vauxhall Bridge in 1816, and the roof of St Pancras Station, which opened during the reign of Queen Victoria in 1868.

POTTERY MANUFACTURE

In 1748, André Planche, the son of French Huguenot refugees, settled in Derby and began to manufacture small pottery figures. In 1756, he went into partnership with a local banker named John Health and with William Duesbury, a porcelain decorator, to produce bone china tableware. Planche returned to London with his family but Health and Duesbury continued with their enterprise. The porcelain that was made at the Nottingham Road factory graced fashionable tables across the country and was known as Derby Porcelain.

In 1764, Duesbury introduced new techniques for transfer printing. In 1773, the business opened a showroom in Covent Garden, London. Two years later, the company received the patronage of King George III and became known as Crown Derby. The porcelain remained popular throughout the Victorian period, and in 1890 Queen Victoria appointed the firm as 'Manufacturers of porcelain to Her Majesty'. The warrant added the Royal to Crown Derby, which is still manufactured at Derby.

HIGHWAY ROBBERY

Despite improvements to the roads, journey times usually remained long, and even hazardous. In Derbyshire, the most notorious example of unwary travellers meeting an untimely end occurred in 1758, when a pair of eloping lovers, Allan and Clara, were butchered by robbers.

The couple were making their way to the Church of the Peak Forest, the Derbyshire equivalent of Gretna Green, where they could marry without the legal need for banns. They travelled from Castleton via the Winnats Pass, where they were attacked and killed for their possessions. Their murderers hid the bodies in an old mine shaft, where the skeletons were alleged to have been discovered in 1768. History has long since turned to legend. There are tales of the gang meeting untimely and violent ends; the sound of Allan and Clara begging for mercy on dark and stormy nights; even a fine red leather saddle on display in the Speedwell Cavern Museum, Castleton, which is said to have belonged to Clara.

Elsewhere in the Peak District, Black Harry, a Tideswell man, robbed the pack horse trains between Tideswell and Bakewell before being captured and executed at Derby.

His cadaver was gibbeted at Wardlow Mires near Buxton, where his remains were a warning to other would-be robbers. He is recalled at Black Harry Gate near Stoney Middleton and the Black Harry trails near Longstone Edge.

CANAL MANIA

The costs of transporting raw materials and finished goods were high. James Brindley, the father of so-called 'canal mania', who oversaw the construction of England's first canals, was born at Tunstead near Buxton in 1716. Today a drinking fountain erected to his memory can be found on the main road at Wormhill. Brindley, the son of an agricultural labourer with no formal education, was apprenticed to a millwright in Macclesfield when he was 17. Having completed his apprenticeship, he moved to Leek in Staffordshire, where he set up business as an engineer and millwright. Still unable to read and write, he committed all his designs for steam engines and pumps for mines to memory.

In 1759, the 3rd Duke of Bridgewater commissioned Brindley to oversee the construction of the Bridgewater Canal. When it opened in 1761, the new canal reduced the cost of transporting coal to Manchester by half. The next twenty years saw industrialists, merchants and members of the nobility investing in canals, which opened up new markets, increased the volume of goods being transported and reduced costs.

In 1766, an Act of Parliament gave permission for the Trent and Mersey Canal, which linked the River Trent in Derbyshire to the River Mersey, connecting the ports of Hull on the east coast with Liverpool in the west. The Staffordshire pottery manufacturer Josiah Wedgewood met the costs of the project, engineered by Brindley, recognising the potential of a coast-to-coast network for his business. The canal, featuring seventy-six locks and five tunnels, took ten years to build, finally opening in 1777, although it ran from Shardlow, 8 miles south-east of Derby, towards Stafford from 1770 onwards.

In Derbyshire, it was necessary to engineer forty locks to join the Trent to the canal at Wilden Ferry near Shardlow. The inland port became increasingly important as the Industrial Revolution gathered pace. Shardlow was known as 'Little Liverpool' because of the number of shipments it handled. By the 1840s, with the coming of the railways, its heyday was over. Today, together with Stourbridge, it is the only intact inland port and canal village in Britain.

Brindley did not live to see the Grand Trunk, as he called the project, completed. He died at the end of September 1772, having allegedly been soaked by a rainstorm and then slept in his drenched clothing, resulting in a fatal chill. Hugh Henshall, Brindley's brother-in-law, continued work on Derbyshire's canal system. An ambitious network of waterways included the Chesterfield Canal and the Cromford Canal.

The Chesterfield Canal was built in 1777, enabling coal and iron to be transported much more efficiently. At Whittington, in Chesterfield, the glass-making industry benefitted from the delivery of sand from King's Lynn rather than having to use local silicas. To the south of the county, the Erewash Canal received its Act of Parliament in 1777, overseen by John Varley. It took two years to build at the cost of £21,000, and was built to transport coal from Long Eaton in Nottinghamshire to Langley Mill in the Amber Valley. The Nutbrook Canal, which was completed in 1796, transported coal from the collieries at Shipley, via Shipley Wharf, on to the Erewash Canal connecting with the River Trent, Nottingham and Langley Mill.

In the north-west of the county, construction started on the Peak Forest Canal close to Whaley Bridge in 1794, with the finances being provided by Richard Arkwright. Barges moved coal but its primary purpose was the transport of limestone from around Dove Holes to the Macclesfield Canal at Marple. The limestone, burned in nearby kilns to make quicklime, had many applications in the developing chemical and steel industries. It was transported to the canal by a gravity-fed tramway to the Bugsworth Basin on the first 6 miles of its journey. The canal ran for 15 miles, rising some 64m over the stretch of just one mile by means of a flight of sixteen locks.

The Derby Canal Act was passed on 7 May 1793 to connect the River Trent at Swarkestone to the Erewash Canal at Sandiacre in Derbyshire, by means of a broad canal capable of taking the largest vessels that plied the Trent. Benjamin Outram, the engineer who also founded the Butterley Company together with wealthy local backers, designed and built the world's first cast-iron aqueduct at Morledge, Derby. It was a single-span structure stretching 13m. The canal's main cargo was coal, and it remained successful until the coming of the railways, when it began to decline even though its owners reduced the tolls levied on the vessels that used the waterway.

PRISONERS OF WAR, GINGERBREAD AND THREE SHIPS

The events of the French Revolution, which began with the storming of the Bastille in Paris in 1789, sent shock waves through Europe. In 1793, the French Republic declared war on Britain, starting a conflict that lasted until 1815.

In 1803, the prisoner-of-war exchange system between England and France broke down. It created a problem of where to keep French prisoners. Officers were imprisoned on a parole system, in which they promised not to try and escape back to France. To make sure that they were unable to help with any French operations on the coast or to communicate with the men they commanded who were not paroled, they were sent to inland market towns. Some were moved to Ashbourne. The first forty-four officers arrived on 17 December 1803, having travelled from custody in Devon. They had all been captured on French warships or merchant vessels. In February 1804, three generals and their entourages were sent to the town. They are likely to have lodged at the Roebuck Inn on St John Street.

It is said that Ashbourne gingerbread was created by a French cook during his time in Derbyshire, and that he shared the recipe with the locals that is still in use today. The number of French prisoners increased until there were 172 of them billeted in the town. The four daughters of the landlord at the Cock Inn on Dig Street all married paroled officers. In 1812 the government tried to prevent weddings with prisoners taking place, but St Oswald's Church celebrated two further marriages.

Chesterfield also became a parole town. Like every other parolee, the officers sent there were given their freedom on the understanding that they were only permitted to travel within a mile of the town and had to be back in their quarters by eight in the evening, when a curfew bell known as the 'Frenchman's bell' was sounded. There was some laxity in the rules. Wingerworth Hall was slightly more than a mile from Chesterfield but Sir Windsor Hunloke, its owner and a Catholic, often invited officers to dine and use his private chapel. It was said that the mile stone was removed from the road on the way to Wingerworth and replaced beyond the hall. As the war continued and Wellington found success against the French in Spain, more prisoners joined those in custody in Chesterfield. By 1810 the town was home to 400 prisoners. The officers received an allowance for their keep but they added to their income by offering language lessons, drawing and music. It was also said that the French prisoners introduced the industry of silk hat-making to the town, while others, adept at carving, created models of the men-of-war that they served upon from wood, bone and hair. Four of the prisoners were surgeons and offered their skills for free to the poor of Chesterfield. By 1814 most of the prisoners of war had gone home, taking, in some instances, their English brides with them, while a few remained in Derbyshire. Part of the churchyard in Chesterfield is known as Frenchman's Quarter.

There were widespread celebrations across Derbyshire for each of Britain's victories, but it was not until 1866 that the

Wellington Monument on Baslow Edge in the Peak District was erected as a tribute to the duke for his victory at Waterloo. The work was commissioned by the 7th Duke of Devonshire's surgeon, Dr Edward Mason Wrench, who felt that a memorial was needed to balance the 3m-tall monument dedicated to Admiral Nelson on Birchen Edge, which had been in place since 1810.

The gritstone column topped by a ball commemorating Nelson's achievement overlooks Baslow. It was placed there by John Brightman, in memory of the admiral following his death and victory at the Battle of Trafalgar in 1805. The three large rocky outcrops next to the monument bear the names of three of Nelson's ships: the Victory, Defiance and Royal Soverin (sic). The first was Nelson's flagship and the vessel upon which he died, while HMS *Sovereign* served as Admiral Collingwood's flagship. HMS *Defiance*, a 74-gun ship of the line, was also at Trafalgar, commanded by Captain Durham. It became famous when his master's mate, James 'Jack' Spratt, dived into the sea with his cutlass between his teeth before boarding, single handed, the French vessel *L'Aigle*.

Luddites and the Pentrich Rising: Revolutionary Derbyshire

Derbyshire faced a severe economic crisis as the Napoleonic wars came to an end. Machine breaking spilled from Nottinghamshire into Derbyshire, fuelled by low wages and the employment of unapprenticed workers producing shoddy goods.

In 1811, 400 men from villages around Pentrich and South Wingfield marched on Crich. The Luddites, as they were known, were named after General Ludd, the mysterious figurehead of textile workers across the country. They intended to break wide frames that were used to make cheap 'cut ups' stockings, made from straight pieces of fabric and then sewn together rather than being made from shaped fabric in one piece by skilled workers. From Crich, the Luddites advanced to Nottingham, expecting to join with other radicals breaking stocking and lace frames. Instead of a revolution there was a rout. More than eighty of them were arrested. Three were hanged and another fourteen transported to Australia.

Tensions escalated as taxes continued to rise. To make matters even worse, the government passed a law in March 1815 that restricted the import of cheap corn to keep bread prices high. In 1816, the harvest failed completely in many parts of Britain. In Derbyshire, as the cost of bread continued to rise, the price of iron ore slumped and engineering companies laid off their workers.

Fearful of a revolution of the kind that had happened in France, the government set up a network of spies. One of them, William Oliver, was sent to Derby as an agent provocateur. It was his task to identify men agitating for political reform. He visited the White Horse Inn at Pentrich, 13 miles north-east of Derby, where he encountered Jeremiah Brandreth, an unemployed stocking knitter, who incited his listeners to violence at the meetings held there. Brandreth was associated with men suspected of machinery breaking. He promised his listeners money, beer and bread if they joined in the rising of which he was a part. Nottingham and Derby were to be attacked, arms seized, and the protesters would march on London where a new government would provide work and food.

On the night of 6 June 1817, the Pentrich men marched via the Butterley Ironworks to Ripley, continuing to Codnor and Langley Mill before being routed at Giltbrook, 6 miles north-west of Nottingham, by the Derbyshire Yeomanry and 15th Hussars. Brandreth and the other ringleaders, William Turner, Isaac Ludlam and George Weightman, were arrested. Three hundred jurymen and 208 witnesses were summoned to the special assizes in Derby to hear the case of treason against the men on 15 October 1817.

Most of the forty-six prisoners on trial were condemned to transportation, but a worse fate awaited the men accused of leading the conspiracy. Between 18 and 25 October, Jeremiah

Brandreth, William Turner and Isaac Ludlam were all sentenced to hanging, drawing and quartering. The Prince Regent signed the warrant but the medieval element of quartering was remitted. Instead, they would be hanged and drawn before being beheaded, becoming the last people in Britain to be beheaded as a means of execution.

On 7 November, the three men were fetched to a scaffold erected in front of Derby Gaol. The three men attested that William Oliver, the government spy, had lured them into rebellion, and then they were hanged before being butchered on a block built specially for the occasion. Among the crowd watching was the poet, Shelley. The government maintained that Oliver was an informant, but even the prime minister, Lord Liverpool, agreed that the spy had gone further than was proper in encouraging the plotters. They might not have progressed beyond talking had the agent not provoked them to action.

REFORM RIOTS

Industrial towns continued to grow but the population change was not reflected by parliamentary representation. Besides which, only 5 per cent of the populace were able to vote. In 1831, the House of Commons voted on a Reform Bill that would enable more people to vote at elections, but when it was put before the Lords the bill was defeated.

News of the defeat arrived in Derby at 7 p.m. on 8 October. Men who would have benefitted from new voting rights rioted and smashed the windows of the town's leading men, who objected to the idea of more people having a say in the way the country was run. The army arrived and the Riot Act was read in the marketplace, ordering the protesters to disperse. In the fighting that followed, shots were fired and several men were injured. By 12 October, Derby was quiet once more, even if the prison was a little more full than usual.

The Derby Spring Assizes of 1832 saw eleven men tried for their part in October's riots and for breaking into Derby's jail, where they freed William Keeling, a convicted felon. Nine of the men were released but two were convicted and transported to Australia.

WHO'S WHO IN GEORGIAN DERBYSHIRE?

Sir Richard Arkwright, a self-made made man from humble beginnings in Preston, Lancashire, was one of the founders of the Industrial Revolution along with Jedediah Strutt. His work with John Kay, a watchmaker, resulted in the design of the world's first mechanised cotton spinning frame that almost anyone could operate. Arkwright's workforce was largely semi-skilled and his mills at Cromford and Wirksworth were the first to employ a modern mass-production factory system. Arkwright chose to live in Cromford and commissioned a grand house, Willersley Castle, overlooking the Derwent Valley, when he was knighted in 1786. It was still incomplete when he died in 1792. He was buried in the churchyard at Cromford.

Robert Bakewell began working in Derbyshire for Thomas Coke of Melbourne Hall in 1706. The master ironsmith built an arbour known as 'the Birdcage' before moving to Derby, where he set up a forge. His elaborate iron gates at Derby Cathedral and elsewhere ensured his reputation.

The dukes of Devonshire were astute politicians and Derbyshire's principal landowners. They served as members of parliament as well as on the Privy Council, and had succeeded the Talbots, Earls of Shrewsbury, to the Lord Lieutenancy of Derbyshire, which meant that they represented the monarchy in the county and were responsible for organising its local militia for the defence of the realm. In 1745, the 3rd Duke of Devonshire raised the Derbyshire Blues militia in support of King George II. The 4th Duke, a Whig politician like his father, was Britain's prime minister from November 1756 until May 1757, but his influence declined with the accession of George III, who did not trust him. In 1762, he resigned as Derbyshire's Lord Lieutenant. He died two years later and was succeeded by his son, William, who like most of the dukes before him was married to a wife who brought money, estates and influence to the Cavendish family.

Lady Georgiana Spencer, Duchess of Devonshire. William Cavendish, 5th Duke of Devonshire, married Lady Georgina Spencer in 1774. She was descended from John Churchill, 1st Duke of Marlborough, and his wife, the redoubtable Lady Sarah Jennings.

The duke seemed indifferent to his beautiful young wife, who needed love and affection to thrive. Lady Elizabeth Foster, the duke's mistress, lived with the couple on good terms with Georgiana. Both women raised their children in the same nursery. It was acceptable for a man to take a mistress and it did not matter that the duchess was deeply unhappy. During the 1780s, Georgiana's gambling became a problem as her losses and the subsequent debts mounted up. By the time the duchess became pregnant with her eldest son she owed one creditor £3,000, and she did not dare tell her husband the true extent of her gambling debts. However, with the birth of a son, named after his father, on 21 May 1790, she hoped that all would be forgiven and the duke would clear her debts, which amounted to £60,000.

Georgiana was soon pregnant again but on this occasion the father was Charles Grey, who would one day become Britain's prime minister. Cavendish cut off Georgiana's allowance and she went abroad to Aix-en-Provence, where she gave birth to her daughter, Eliza. The child eventually found a home with her paternal grandparents, Lord and Lady Grey, in Northumberland. The duchess was permitted to return to Chatsworth.

She went on to have several affairs, an addiction to gambling and was something of a fashion icon. She once wore a model ship in full sail in her hair. Her friends included Marie Antoinette and the Prince Regent. The family divided their time between Chatsworth and Devonshire House on Piccadilly in London. While the duke spent time in his gentlemen's clubs, the duchess campaigned on behalf of the Whig Party and became a leading socialite.

The Cavendishes still owned Buxton, but, unlike Bath, it was not part of England's social scene. The duke bankrolled the rebuilding of Buxton, turning it into a fashionable watering hole that might compete with Bath, in the hope that his duchess would spend more time in Derbyshire. The 'Great Stables' was finished in 1779. It provided stabling for up to 120 horses, as well as quarters for the servants of the men and women who came to stay to take the restorative waters of Buxton's spa. It was only in 1880, by which time the building was a charity hospital for the poor visiting Buxton to take a water cure, that its magnificent dome was added. At more than 45m in diameter, it was the largest unsupported structure of its kind in the world. The duke's statue can be found outside the Crescent, which was completed in 1789.

Erasmus Darwin, the grandfather of Charles Darwin, moved to Derby in 1783 from Lichfield. Soon after his arrival he formed the Derby Philosophical Society with his friend Joseph Wright, among others. Its aim was to extend scientific understanding. He died in 1802 at Breadsall Priory and was buried at the nearby church.

Joseph Wright, of Derby, was born in Derby and educated at the Free Grammar School there. He became a self-taught artist before studying at the Royal Academy in London. He returned to Derbyshire, earning money by painting portraits and landscapes, including Dovedale. He is most famous for his interpretation of the Enlightenment, the birth of modern science and the Industrial Revolution. His work, notable for its innovative use of light and dark, turned him into one of the most important artists of the eighteenth century. He died in 1797 and was buried at St Alkmund's Church. Today his memorial can be found inside Derby Cathedral. The largest collection of his work in the world can be found in the Derby Museum and Art Gallery. His birthplace, on Irongate, is remembered by a spherical astrolabe.

7

VICTORIAN DERBYSHIRE

By 1836, three different companies, the Midlands Counties Railway, the North Midland Railway and the Birmingham and Derby Junction Railway, gained parliamentary consent for lines to Derby. In 1839, the town opened one of the largest stations in the country, accommodating all three enterprises. In 1844, the three railway companies amalgamated to form the Midland Railway.

Derby grew as a centre for the rail industry. As well as the town being a hub for administration and building the rolling stock, the railway revived Derby's textile industry because of a demand for uniforms. The expansion of the railway line to serve London and as far north as Carlisle benefited

Derbyshire's other industries, and changed the fortunes of towns in the Peak District. The railway reached Matlock in 1849, Ashbourne in 1852, and Buxton in 1863. The arrival of train lines made the Peak District accessible to middle-class day trippers from nearby towns, including Manchester and Sheffield, who wished to emulate the queen. Princess Victoria, as she was then, visited Matlock Bath in 1832 and again in 1844, when she stayed at Chatsworth House as a guest of the Duke of Devonshire.

COAL IS KING

Railways made it economical to send coal from Derbyshire to London. The Butterley Company, whose headquarters were at Ripley, owned foundries at Butterley and Codnor, limestone works at Crich and, by the 1870s, fifteen collieries. The pattern was repeated in Chesterfield by Richard Barrow and his brother, who owned the ironworks at Staveley. By 1913, Derbyshire's coal mines would be producing 18 million tons of coal per year.

The work of a collier was dirty, difficult and dangerous. In 1861, at Clay Cross, twenty-three miners were killed when the mine flooded. Despite a decline in the number of fatal accidents, in part thanks to the appointment of an Inspector of Mines in 1850, roof cave-ins and disasters continued. Among them, at Renishaw Park Colliery, first sunk by J & G Wells Ltd on land leased from the Sitwell family of Renishaw Hall, an explosion in January 1871 killed twenty-five men and two boys.

NOSE TO THE GRINDSTONE?

Derbyshire produced more mill stones than any other area of the country. They came in pairs and were known as 'Peaks' by the millers who used them to make flour. The stone at the bottom remains stationary but the top stone turns to create a grinding action, powered by water, wind or steam. The market's decline began in the eighteenth century with the import of 'French stones' made from a composite of chert and cement. They produced a finer ground white flour than the Peak stones. The introduction of high-speed steel rollers that replaced more traditional windmills, like the one at Heage, or post mills, like the Cat and Fiddle Mill at Dale Abbey near Ilkeston, ended Derbyshire's production of mill stones but left them scattered across the gritstone edges of the Peak District in varying degrees of completion.

Gritstone served other purposes besides agriculture. In Sheffield, the cutlery and knife industries required grind stones for sharpening steel blades. Prior to the Victorian period, Hathersage had five mills sharpening the points of pins and needles for the textile industry. A third type of stone, known as an edge runner, was mounted on an axle and used to crush hard materials including lead ore, pigments and glass.

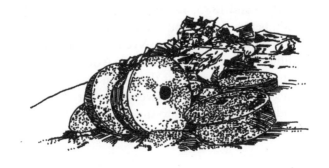

DERBYSHIRE'S LAST LEAD MINE

The Magpie Mine near Sheldon was so successful that there were disputes with neighbouring mines about who had the rights to work the veins in the area. On occasion, miners from opposing mines would light fires underground to force one another out. In 1833, three miners from Maypitt Mine were suffocated by the fumes and twenty-four men from the Magpie Mine were put on trial for murder. All of them were acquitted because it was impossible to identify the men responsible for setting the fire. It was said that the widows of the murdered men cursed the mine that had killed their husbands. The disputes led to the closure of the mine for a time.

In 1839, it was bought by John Taylor, a Cornish mining engineer. He introduced shift working as well as installing a new pumping engine and winding equipment. By the 1860s most of the county's lead mines were closed as the value of lead fell and the cost of production rose. The expense of steam engines to drain shafts when they reached the water table was too great for most mine owners. The Magpie Mine was an exception, even though its main shaft is over 200m deep. In 1869, John Taylor installed a new Cornish pumping engine to replace the earlier mechanism, as well as machinery for winding the ore to the surface.

Between 1873 and 1883, a sough, or drainage channel, was built to drain between four and six million gallons of water a day from the mine into the River Wye near Ashford, but the financial difficulties of keeping the mine working proved too great and it closed the year that the sough was completed. It was reopened briefly during the twentieth century but closed in 1958, and was then taken into the care of the Peak District Mines Historical Society.

SOCIAL REFORM

The Poor Law Act of 1601 required individual parishes to care for their paupers. Local people served as overseers, collecting money through the Poor Rate to distribute to the needy. The emphasis was always on requiring people to work rather than to claim relief. During the eighteenth century, several parishes established workhouses; the Old Parish Poorhouse in Winster is one of them. It opened in 1744 and could accommodate forty or so inmates, reflecting the relative importance of the parish at the time.

In March 1834, the Poor Law Amendment Act was introduced. Provision for the poor in their own homes, or outdoor relief, would only be made to those who were too old or too sick to work. In future the poor would be forced to live in workhouses, where they would be made to work for their keep. Parishes banded together to form unions under the control of a board of guardians.

In Derbyshire there were nine different unions. Chesterfield was part of the Ashover Union, which formed voluntarily in 1767. One of the criticisms of the Poor Law commissioner who visited the workhouse there in 1832 was that inmates were not required to work. The new union formed in 1837, before it was legally required to do so. Its governors decided that Chesterfield should have a new workhouse capable of holding 300 paupers and purchased land on the Newbold Road. The resulting building was designed by architects George Gilbert Scott and William Moffatt. The three-storey red-brick accommodation block was divided into men's accommodation in the east and women's to the west. Even the exercise yard was segregated. As well as a porter's lodge, boardroom and school, there was a laundry, workshops and an infirmary. Chesterfield's poor were required to grind bones, break limestone and pick oakum. This involved removing very hard tar from ropes. The fibres had to be teased apart strand by strand so that it could be resold to ship builders to use as wadding to make wooden vessels watertight.

Belper, the largest town in Victorian Derbyshire apart from Derby, formed a union composed of thirty-four parishes. Its purpose-built accommodation, also designed by Scott and Moffatt, opened its doors in 1838. Facilities included cells for tramps who had to pay for their night's shelter by breaking stone into pieces small enough to pass through a metal grille.

THE FIRST PUBLIC PARK

In 1840, Joseph Strutt, the youngest son of Jedediah Strutt, donated the Arboretum to Derby. It was England's first publicly owned recreational park. Strutt, a Unitarian who believed that with wealth came social responsibility, was grateful to the working people of Derby for the part they played in establishing his family's fortunes. He wanted to provide them with somewhere they might enjoy the outdoors. The park, designed by the botanist John Loudon, was open to all and free to enter on Wednesday and Sunday. The admission, paid by those who could afford it, ensured that the park was maintained.

Strutt's social conscience and the emphasis upon serving Derby's population as a whole helped inspire Frederick Olmsted's vision for Central Park in New York, which won a contest for the park's design in 1858. Olmsted, who visited England in 1850, returned to Derby in 1859 to see the Arboretum for himself.

THE FORMATION OF DERBYSHIRE COUNTY COUNCIL

In 1888, local government took responsibility for turnpike roads, and the following year Derbyshire County Council was formed from eighty councillors of whom the majority were elected, rather than appointed to their posts as was the case previously.

The boundaries of the county also changed. A block of parishes that belonged to Derbyshire were transferred to Leicestershire in 1897, and the village of Appleby Magna was divided between the two counties, while other parishes were transferred to Staffordshire with the boundary between the two counties indicated by the course of the Rive Dove. Derby, an ancient county brough, was administered independently from the county council.

WHO'S WHO IN VICTORIAN DERBYSHIRE?

Catherine Booth was born in Ashbourne in 1829. Her parents, Sarah and John Mumford, were both Methodists, and Catherine received a Christian upbringing. She married William Booth in 1855 and together they co-founded the Salvation Army. Catherine was an early advocate of female preachers and the importance of women's ministry. She also campaigned for better working conditions and pay for women. She is commemorated by a plaque marking the house where she was born and a memorial bust in the recreation ground at Ashbourne.

Thomas Cook was born at Melbourne in 1808. He began work, at 10 years old, as an assistant market gardener. In 1841, he took a group of temperance campaigners on an excursion from Leicester to Loughborough. Each of the 845 people he escorted paid 1s for the return journey by train. In 1851, he escorted 150,000 people to see the Great Exhibition in London. Four years later he planned his first trip abroad. He went on to form Thomas Cook and Son, which went on to become a global travel agent. In 1891, at Melbourne, he commissioned the building of fourteen cottages for poor Baptists.

George Curzon, 1st Marquess Curzon of Kedleston, was part of a family who arrived in Derbyshire with William the Conqueror. He went to India in 1891 and, in 1899, was appointed Viceroy. He returned to England after the death of Queen Victoria.

Florence Nightingale spent some of her childhood holidays in the family's Derbyshire home, Lea Hurst, near Matlock. She was there in October 1854 when the appalling conditions of the Crimean War made national headlines. Eighteen months later, Nightingale, a trained nurse, led a group of women to the hospitals at Scutari to assist with the casualties sent from the battlefields. Her advice on making hospitals hygienic and airier led to the rebuilding of Derbyshire Infirmary in 1891, as well as its earlier 1869 remodelling. There is a statue of the Lady with the Lamp outside the former Derbyshire Royal Infirmary on London Road, and on the corner of East Street and St Peter's Street. The latter was placed there when the building was built in 1912, along with others of Derby's historic figures.

Joseph Paxton, head gardener at Chatsworth, was only 20 years of age when the 6th Duke of Devonshire, Georgina's son, appointed him to the post in 1823. It was his job to redesign the garden and relocate what remained of the old village of Edensor when the duke gave orders for a new road to be built. In 1832, Paxton built a new greenhouse at Chatsworth. In 1836, he built the Great Conservatory, which was heated by eight boilers and 7 miles of iron pipe. His designs would inspire Crystal Palace in London in 1851. He also corresponded with George Stephenson, the engineer, about the best way to grow straight cucumbers. In Derbyshire, though, he is more famous for Chatsworth's Emperor Fountain, which was built in 1843 when it seemed likely that Tsar Nicholas I of Russia might visit. The resulting jet of water is up to 90m high.

George Stephenson moved with his wife Elizabeth to Tapton House near Chesterfield in 1837, when he was commissioned to supervise the building of the North Midland Railway through the town. The line ran between Derby and Leeds. He formed the Clay Cross Company to take advantage of the rich seams of coal in the area, which he recognised would find a ready market with the railways. Within a few years he employed more than 1,000 people in his mines at Tapton, Brimington and Newbold. At the same time, he used the station at Ambergate to transport lime from the quarries at Crich for processing in a bank of twenty limekilns there.

When Stephenson died in 1848, he was buried in the Holy Trinity Church, Newbold Road, Chesterfield, next to his wife near the altar. A stained-glass window was installed in his memory. Today, a life-sized statue of the engineer can be found standing outside Chesterfield's railway station, holding a measuring compass in one hand and a model of Locomotion No.1, better known as Rocket, in the other.

8

THE WORLD AT WAR

In 1906, Rolls-Royce was formed as a company to build quality cars. Work began on their Derby factory in April 1907 on a 1½-acre site at Nightingale Road, which opened on 9 July 1908. The town was able to offer skilled labour at a lower price than Manchester, or elsewhere, as well as the ready availability of raw materials and forges to make steel. The 400-strong workforce was responsible for the production of the iconic Silver Ghost, which was sent all over the world. Customers included the Tsar of Russia.

WORLD WAR ONE

On 28 July 1914, the assassination of Archduke Franz Ferdinand of Austria and his wife triggered a chain of events that led, on 4 August, to Britain declaring war on Germany. Three days after war was declared, the famous recruiting poster depicting Lord Kitchener and the words 'Your Country Needs You' was circulated and the territorial battalions of the Sherwood Foresters (Notts and Derby) were called back to their depots in Chesterfield and Derby for mobilisation.

In Derby, the railway industry began working for the war effort, turning its production lines over to howitzers and shells, ambulance trains, army service vehicles and gun carriage parts. In 1914, Rolls-Royce developed an armoured car, turning all its available Silver Ghost chassis over to its production. In 1915, the company developed the Eagle, the world's first reliable aero-engine, and began to manufacture them at their Nightingale Road factory for the Royal Flying Corps.

ZEPPELINS OVER DERBY

On 31 January 1916, nine German Zeppelins mounted a raid on Derby and other Midlands towns. It is thought that their intended target was Liverpool but navigational errors meant that in the early evening they passed over Derby, which was clearly visible from the air because there were no blackout regulations in place. One bomb landed on the Rolls-Royce site while others, which failed to explode, fell on the gasworks.

THE POISON PLOT OF 1917

On 30 January 1917, Alice Wheeldon and her family were arrested in Derby. They were all accused of plotting to murder Prime Minister David Lloyd George. Alice believed that the charge was trumped up because she and her family were conscientious objectors. Since 1916, when conscription to the armed services was imposed, she and her daughter Hettie, a teacher in Ilkeston who shared her mother's anti-war sympathies, advised men who sought to gain exemption from military service.

It was true that Alice was a vociferous member of the No-Conscription Fellowship and that she was an active suffragette as well as being a socialist. Her beliefs at a time when Britain was at war were viewed as dangerous radicalism. However, the case against the Wheeldon family was based entirely upon the evidence of a man called Alec Gordon, who initially claimed to be a conscientious objector on the run from the authorities. On 27 December 1916, he arrived at Alice's second-hand clothes shop on Pear Tree Road seeking shelter.

Gordon introduced Mrs Wheeldon to a man who called himself 'Comrade Bert', another conscientious objector. Comrade Bert claimed to have links with the labour movement in London. Gordon also promised to help the cause of men refusing to fight if she could provide poison to kill dogs that he said guarded the detention camp where conscientious objectors were held. Alice obtained four phials of poison from her son-in-law, Alfred Mason, married to Winnie Wheeldon, a chemist employed by Southampton University. The poisons despatched through the post were curare and strychnine.

Winnie wrote to her mother asking her to be careful about what she wrote and to use an old suffragette code. The warning was too late. The family's letters to one another would be used as evidence against them when the case came to court. Their correspondence was hostile to the war and to Lloyd George, but none of it suggested that the family were considering assassinating the prime minister.

A trial began at the Derby Guildhall but was moved to the Old Bailey in London, where the case was heard on 6 March 1917. The accusation against the Wheeldons rested on the testimony of Alex Gordon, who did not appear as a witness at the trial either for the defence or the prosecution. His real name was William Rickard and he, together with Comrade Bill, an alias for Herbert Booth, were agents working for the Parliamentary Military Security Department known as PMS2. It was the role of the sector to protect munitions factories from sabotage. It was also responsible for gathering information about the labour movement and to infiltrate any groups it came across. It seems likely that PMS2 was used, on this occasion, to prevent the Wheeldon family from its work supporting conscientious objectors.

Whatever the truth of the matter might have been, Alice, her two daughters and her son-in-law, Alfred Mason, were found guilty of attempted murder. Only Alice's unmarried daughter

Hettie was acquitted. Alice was given a sentence of ten years, but served only ten months before being released from Holloway Prison on licence at the request of Lloyd George. By then she was suffering from heart failure as a result of an eight-day hunger strike she subjected herself to following the Court of Criminal Appeal's rejection of her case. She died from influenza in 1919.

The work of PMS2 ceased shortly after Alice's case came to court. Gordon's methods were questioned in the House of Commons and Ramsay MacDonald, the MP for Leicester, demanded to know who he really was. In 2022, the Criminal Cases Review Commission stated that the case was too old to refer to the Court of Appeal but noted the real possibility that the three convictions would be overturned.

DERBYSHIRE REMEMBERS AND IS THANKFUL

War memorials became a common sight throughout Derbyshire in the aftermath of the Great War. Almost every community grieved for, and remembered, young men who went to war but did not return home. The Sherwood Foresters lost 11,410 men between 1914 and 1918. In 1923, to commemorate their loss, Crich Stand, in the form of a lighthouse, was built in Derbyshire on Crich Hill, 286m above sea level. The location is said to have been the site of a beacon fire that signalled the sighting of the Spanish Armada in the English Channel in 1588. On a clear day it is even possible to make out Lincoln Cathedral, which is more than 50 miles away.

Bradbourne in the Peak District, a so-called Doubly Thankful Village, saw all its men return safely after both wars, including one man who was born in Derbyshire but who emigrated to Australia before 1914. There are only fifteen Doubly Thankful Villages in the whole country. Bradbourne still gives thanks every year for its good fortune.

ASHBOURNE ROYAL SHROVETIDE FOOTBALL

On 28 February 1922, Princess Mary, the daughter of King George V, married Viscount Lascelles at Westminster Abbey. It was Shrove Tuesday. Ashbourne's Shrovetide Football committee sent a special Shrovetide football to the couple as a wedding gift, and in return the king granted the annual match, the pre-fix 'Royal'. In 1928, Mary's brother, the Prince of Wales, later Edward VIII, was welcomed to Ashbourne, where he started that year's fixture.

The game has its roots in medieval mass football, but the earliest mention of Ashbourne's match is 1683. The contest,which still includes the whole of the town, is certainly unlikely to have been allowed during Oliver Cromwell's Commonwealth. Attempts were also made by the Victorians to stop the practice, under the terms of the Highways Act, but they too were unsuccessful in ending the tradition.

The goals are around 3 miles apart and the teams, known as 'upp'ards' and 'down'ards', can be of any size depending on whether the players were born north or south of the Henmore Brook that sits between the two goals. The leather ball can be kicked, carried or thrown once the game begins. This is done by 'turning up', throwing the ball into the air. The ball disappears into a 'hug' of players all struggling for possession. After several hours one team or other will successfully move the ball within sight of one of the two former mills that mark the goals. A player must jump into the river and hit the ball against a mill stone, mounted on a plinth, three times, to score a goal. The game pauses at 10 p.m. and resumes the next day.

A LOCAL DERBY

During the eighteenth century there was a similar game played in the streets of Derby. The young men from the parish of All Saints challenged those from St Peter's. In 1848, troops had to be called upon to restore order during the fighting that followed a match. Since then, a 'local Derby' has been a phrase used to describe any match between two neighbouring teams likely to excite strong emotions.

MASS TRESPASS

On 24 April 1932, hundreds of men and women from the surrounding towns met at the village of Hayfield on the moors leading to Kinder Scout in the Dark Peak area of Derbyshire. It was their intention to walk across the moorlands, in the hands of wealthy private landowners, up to the summit. The rally at Hayfield was overseen by one third of Derbyshire's police force, but the meeting was a ruse to distract the authorities. Hundreds more people set off from Bowden Bridge Quarry for what would become known as the mass trespass on Kinder Scout.

At William Clough, trespassers were confronted by gamekeepers in the employment of local landowners. Scuffles broke out and one of the gamekeepers was injured. The ramblers broke through the gap and met up on the Kinder plateau with another group who began their own walk from Sheffield. On the way back down to Hayfield, six of the trespassers were arrested. They were tried at Derby on charges ranging from trespass to riotous assembly. Five young men were sent to prison, resulting in a groundswell of sympathy that fuelled the right to roam movement and the growing demand for national parks where people might enjoy the countryside.

THE GREAT FLOOD OF 1932

Derby has been flooded on several occasions by the River Trent. The first recorded occasion was in 1673. The town was so badly flooded in 1842 that a culvert was built on Markeaton Brook to prevent it happening again. The depth of the flood is indicated by an iron plaque on the wall of the former Wardwick Tavern on Victoria Street. This level was exceeded in May 1932, when more than 7cm of rain fell in thirty-six hours and the flood defences failed.

Water surged down the Derwent, ripping Millford Bridge at Belper from its piers before overwhelming Derby. The streets were like rivers, with water smashing plate-glass windows and flooding shops as well as the police and fire stations. Power failed when the torrent engulfed the electricity station. A gas main fractured by the waters exploded the following day, 12 May, injuring eleven people. Afterwards, the County Borough of Derby commissioned two new flood relief culverts and upgraded the town's sewerage system.

WORLD WAR TWO:
BARRAGE BALLOONS AND STARFISH DECOYS

Derby's schoolchildren were evacuated into the countryside to the north and east of the town and blackout regulations enforced as soon as war was declared on 3 September 1939. The county's local regiment, the Sherwood Foresters, was sent to France. In May 1940, while workmen removed road signs in case of invasion, relations of the men serving overseas could only hope that their loved ones would make it home safely. Derbyshire men evacuated off the beaches at Dunkirk in June were sent to Singapore, North Africa and Greece in the years that followed.

The London Midland and Scottish Railway's factory in Derby began to make Hurricane fighter planes. The locomotive works manufactured tanks, and other local foundries, including the Stanton Ironworks, produced a range of wartime necessities including gun turrets, shell and bomb casings, and parts for air-raid shelters. Derby once again became a target for German bombing raids, in part because the Rolls-Royce factory made Merlin aircraft engines for Spitfires and Hurricanes.

Thirty barrage balloons floated over the town. Anti-aircraft guns were stationed on the racecourse and at Markeaton Park in order to offer some protection to the town and its vital war work. Because of the importance of Rolls-Royce to the Royal Air Force, Derby became one of seven cities identified in the aftermath of the night-time bombing of Coventry in November 1940 as being in need of immediate protection. Operation Starfish created a night-time decoy site to look, from the air, as though Derby was in flames. As soon as German bombers began a raid, the decoy site was set alight. It was essential that any fires in Derby were quickly contained and that blackout was strictly maintained if the ploy was to work. The intention of the dummy fires was to divert further waves of bombers from their target and for the ordnance they carried to land harmlessly in the countryside.

It was not always possible to prevent aircraft from finding their targets. On the evening of 15 January 1941, the Midland Railway Station was hit as well as several factories and homes. Twenty people were killed and more than 1,650 people left homeless. The following year, on 27 July, a single Dornier Do 217 aircraft bombed the Rolls-Royce factory, killing twelve of its workers as they changed shifts and another eleven people who lived nearby. Even so, the town escaped relatively unscathed. By 1944, Derby was considered safe enough to take evacuees from London escaping from doodlebugs and V-2 rockets.

RESERVOIRS AND BOUNCING BOMBS

The Ladybower, Howden and Derwent Reservoirs to the north of the county were built at the beginning of the twentieth century to supply water to Sheffield and the cities of the East Midlands. The largest of the three reservoirs, the Ladybower, was completed in 1944. The spire of St John and

St James in the lost village of Derwent rose above the water, but was finally demolished in 1947.

The Derwent Reservoir became famous when it was used by the Dambusters of 617 Squadron to practise low-flying runs across water in preparation for their raid on the dams of the Ruhr in 1943. They used Barnes Wallis's bombs that bounced across water until they struck their targets, sunk, and then exploded like a depth charge. Today there is a memorial to the crews that flew on the raid on the west tower of the dam.

DERBYSHIRE'S WORST WINTER

The war ended in 1945, but in 1946 the government imposed bread rationing and war-weary Derbyshire folk continued to face difficult times. To make matters worse, the region was hit by one of the worst winters it had ever seen. Snow fell from January until March 1947. Transport networks came to a standstill in the Peak District because of 3m drifts. The snow was piled so high that it reached the upper windows of some properties. Power went off, milk froze in the churns and food was in short supply. In Biggin, near Buxton, villagers shared their dwindling rations with the German prisoners at the nearby prisoner-of-war camp. Elsewhere, people began to burn their furniture in an attempt to stay warm, and a Halifax plane carrying supplies to isolated villages crashed because of poor visibility. Two of its crew are buried in the cemetery at Buxton.

9

MODERN TIMES

Derbyshire's railway network was reduced as industries closed and, during the 1960s, as a consequence of Dr Beeching's rail review. Ilkeston closed its station to passengers in 1950 and the goods service ended in 1960. Like Ashbourne, which lost its station in 1954, the population was forced to rely on road transport. Britain underwent a transport revolution. In 1958, Derby gained a new ring road, followed by the development of a new indoor retail space called the Eagle Centre that included an underground car park. By 1966, car ownership in Derby was only slightly below the national average, and by the 1970s three quarters of all journeys were made by private vehicle.

THE END OF THE OLD INDUSTRIES

Coal production began to decline in Derbyshire as prices fell at the end of the First World War. The exception to this was at the Markham and Butterley collieries, where extra men were employed with investment made in new coal-cutting machinery. By the time the Second World War started in 1939, Markham and Co. had the largest annual output of coal in the country, 19 million tons. The Bolsover Co., with a production of 5 million tons per year, was the third largest but the industry was in need of reorganisation.

Collieries in Derbyshire were nationalised in 1947 along with the gas, electricity, steel and railway companies. Within twenty years, older and shallower pits were worked out and closed down, pit ponies who had spent their lives underground were retired, and the pits that remained often became deeper than ever. The practice of opencast mining was also introduced, changing Derbyshire's landscape, and in many cases damaging it, for generations to come.

Improved safety regulations did not prevent accidents or fatalities. On 26 September 1950, Derbyshire collieries suffered their worst pit disaster when a seam at Creswell, previously part of the Bolsover Colliery Company, caught fire. A belt carrying coal to the pithead tore and became jammed. Friction caused a fire that spread quickly. The pit face was 3½ miles into the mine. Most of the miners on shift that night had no inkling of the developing disaster until the power went off. By then, lack of water pressure meant that little could be done by those on the surface desperately trying to save the lives of the men below ground. Fifty-one miners escaped by the return airway that carried air which had already ventilated the pit back to the surface. When it became clear that no more men would make it to safety, the decision was taken to seal the mine to starve the fire of air. Eighty men died from carbon monoxide poisoning. It was almost eleven months before the last of the bodies was recovered.

By 1993 all the pits in Derbyshire were closed. The last to shut was at Markham Vale. Since then, spoil heaps across the county have been levelled and landscaped. In South Derbyshire, the National Forest is restoring colliery sites, reintroducing mixed woodland and reinstating hedgerows as well as protecting and managing the area's mining heritage. In total the district is home to one third of the National Forest. Tourism and leisure have their own place in Derbyshire's mining legacy. The Five Pits Trail, managed by Derbyshire County Council, which mainly follows the route of the Great Central Railway near Chesterfield, has transformed the industrial landscape around the town since the closure of the Williamthorpe Colliery in 1970 from one of coal to conservation.

MINERAL EXTRACTION TODAY

Limestone has been extracted from around Buxton for centuries. The modern industry is a high-technology one. In 2009, there were thirteen active limestone quarries in the Peak District, including the Tunstead super-quarry in the Chee Valley that produces 5.5 million tonnes of limestone each year. The Lefarge Cement Works at Hope is dominated by the works chimney, which stands 130m tall.

The region is the main area in Britain for the extraction of fluorspar, calcium fluoride, which is used by the chemical industry for plastics, propellants and anaesthetics. It is also an important ingredient in toothpaste. Barytes and calcite are also quarried. Lead is a by-product of the modern industries.

The main processing plant is at Cavendish Mill near Stony Middleton, where the ore is crushed and minerals separated out. As well as fluorite, 20,000 tons of barite are processed at Cavendish Mill and used in a range of industrial products, including the manufacture of paint.

FRIDEN BRICKWORKS

The firm was founded in 1892 to use Derbyshire's silica deposits and clay to make heat-resistant bricks used by the steel industry. It expanded during the first half of the twentieth century, employing 400 men from nearby villages to mine the silica and work in the factory producing the bricks.

Today the workforce is approximately a quarter of the size it once was, but it remains one of the Peak District's largest employers, making alumina refractory bricks and blocks that are exported around the world for use in steel, glass, ceramics, cement and petrochemical industries.

PLANES, TRAINS, AUTOMOBILES AND SUBMARINES

The heavy industry of Derbyshire's past has largely been replaced by modern high-value manufacturing. The county, a hub for engineering excellence, is home to Rolls-Royce, JCB, Bombardier, Toyota and Ferodo. The latter, started by Herbert Frood, has been in Chapel-en-le-Frith since 1902. Herbert Frood began his enterprise by creating cotton brakes for horse-drawn wagons. His became the first company to use asbestos in brake linings and was the first to use alternatives when the dangers of this mineral became apparent.

JCB's Foston factory in the Dove Valley makes diesel engines for JCB vehicles. In 2006, the JCB Dieselmax car achieved a speed of 350mph using engines built in Derbyshire, breaking the diesel land speed record.

The first mainline diesel-electric locomotive in Derby was built in 1947. Ten years later, the town produced its last steam locomotive. Bombardier continues to make trains and rolling stock for Britain's railways and London's underground network. In 2022, the Class 345 trains in service on the Crossrail Elizabeth Line in London were designed and built in Derby.

Rolls-Royce provides the engines for Bombardier's business class jet planes. The company remains a prominent employer in Derby with a focus on the aerospace industry, having developed and built the engines for the world's largest passenger plane in 2005, and a contract with the Royal Navy for the provision of nuclear reactor plants for submarines.

Successful modern firms like Rolls-Royce recognise the importance of research and collaboration. Rolls-Royce and Derby University's engineering department work together on a variety of projects. As well as creating a skilled workforce, the links between research and industry provide new opportunities for Derbyshire's manufacturing future.

Globalisation has increased competition and opened up new markets. Toyota has been manufacturing cars at their Burnaston plant near Derby since 1992. The production line represents a huge investment in modern manufacturing methods, as well as reflecting the way the car industry has changed to meet the environmental challenges of the twenty-first century. In 2007, it rolled the first mass-produced hybrid car in Europe off its lines.

THE PEAK DISTRICT NATIONAL PARK

In 1945, the Peak District was identified as one of six areas recommended for National Park status. In 1950, it became Britain's first National Park, covering 542 square miles, with its headquarters at Bakewell. The task of the park authority is to enhance the area's natural beauty and promote enjoyment for the people visiting it. It also has to accommodate the needs of the 38,000 or so people who call the area home and for whom the region is a working landscape.

A MODERN APPROACH TO OWNERSHIP

Winster Market House, dating to the eighteenth century, was purchased for the National Trust in 1906, making it the first bought by the Trust in Derbyshire. In 1950, when the 10th Duke of Devonshire died unexpectedly, the Cavendish family faced heavy death duty taxes. They chose to transfer possession of Hardwick Hall into the hands of the state to help pay what they owed, and Bess of Hardwick's mansion became part of the Trust's portfolio. The National Trust, which owns property and land throughout the county, aims to look after historic sites, green spaces and the countryside. Today the National Trust, through the work of its local vol-

unteers and fund raisers, continues to look after many of Derbyshire's stately homes, including Kedleston Hall near Derby with its magnificent eighteenth-century interior, and Calke Abbey, which is often described as an 'un-stately' home, as well as maintaining landscapes within the Peak District including restoring ancient peat moorlands. Much of what it does enables visitors, both local and from further afield, to enjoy Derbyshire's countryside and historic buildings.

It is not alone. Chatsworth House reopened its doors to the public in 1949 and a trust that formed in 1981 to care for the house, gardens and park is committed to offering facilities for the benefit of the people who visit it each year. Elvaston Castle, to the south of the county, remained largely uninhabited after the Second World War until it was sold, in 1969, by William Stanhope, 11th Earl of Harrington, to Derbyshire County Council. The castle continued its decline but the council opened the estate to the public in 1970 as Elvaston Castle Country Park, becoming the first country park in England following the Countryside Act of 1968, which gave local authorities the power to establish country parks to make it easier for people living in towns to enjoy outdoor leisure without the need to make long journeys. The council has renovated the castle's formal gardens and improved access to the parkland that surrounds the castle.

The changing use of Derbyshire's countryside and access to its stately homes came with their own problems. By the 1980s the traffic congestion was a real issue, but improved transport networks, car parks, cycle hire schemes and clear information helped relieve visitor pressure. By 2007, the Peak District was better equipped to welcome in excess of 32 million visitors.

WELL DRESSING REVIVAL

Peak District towns and villages developed an extensive calendar of well dressings that are unique to the area during the second half of the twentieth century. The authorities, with an oversight of the tourist economy, were quick to recognise their potential as a day out for visitors.

Dressings involve decorating springs and wells with clay-filled boards illustrated with pictures made from natural materials pressed into the clay. No one is absolutely certain when the tradition began but it is a long-standing one in many places. It is possible that it has its origins in pagan sacrifices made to water gods. In AD 960, the Christian Church forbade the worship of fountains, but the practice appears to have been adopted by the Church as a way of giving thanks for the gift of water. There is mention of well dressing in Tissington in 1348, perhaps to give thanks for the purity of the water in a time when the Black Death was wreaking havoc. The only certainty is that in 1758, Nicholas Hardinge, Clerke of the House of Commons, saw and recorded the sight of the springs at Tissington decorated with garlands. By the end of the century, the *Gentleman's Magazine* was able to write that it was a 'custom from time immemorial' to decorate the springs with flowers every Holy Thursday.

With the passage of time, more places began to dress their own sources of water. In 1840, the Duke of Devonshire paid for the boards that dressed the Market Place Fountain, which was the town's first public supply at Buxton. By the 1850s, the custom extended beyond the Peak District to Derby.

By the end of the twentieth century, more than eighty communities across the Peak District spent several weeks each year creating short-lived but beautiful pictures from petals, seeds and berries on themes ranging from Bible stories to voting rights for women. Visitors often return on a regular basis to tour the decorated water features and take part in the celebrations that accompany them.

A NEW MILLENNIUM

Derbyshire celebrated the new century with fireworks across the county while, at Crich, the millennium beacon was part of a chain of hundreds of beacons across the country. At New Mills, the occasion was marked by opening of the Torrs Millennium Walkway above the River Goyt. The 160m cantilevered walkway, described as a 'steel spider's' web', crosses a previously impassable gorge, celebrating the area's industrial heritage and its natural beauty as well as connecting various long-distance paths.

DERBYSHIRE'S FASTEST SOLO SAILOR TO SAIL AROUND THE WORLD

Yachtswoman Ellen MacArthur from near Matlock hit the headlines in 2005 after spending seventy-one days alone at sea, when she broke the world record for the fastest solo navigation of the globe. The feat is all the more remarkable because landlocked Derbyshire, at 70 miles, is the county furthest from Britain's coast.

DERBYSHIRE AND PROUD

Derbyshire's flag was unveiled for the first time in 2006 after listeners to Radio Derby were invited to design and vote for an emblem that best represented Derbyshire. It depicts a green cross on a blue background representing Derbyshire's countryside and its rivers and reservoirs. The Tudor rose, which has been the county badge since the fifteenth century, is depicted in gold in the middle of the flag. The following year, on 22 September 2007, the county celebrated its first Derbyshire Day, when the flag was flown across the county.

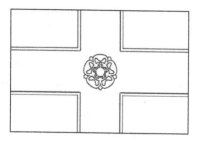

Brexit and Beyond

In 2016, Derbyshire voted to leave the European Union in the Brexit Referendum. The Derbyshire Dales vote was almost identical to the national split with just under 52 per cent voting to leave. Even so, the loss of the UK's biggest trading partner led to some real concerns that Toyota might withdraw from its Burnaston production line. Rolls-Royce and Bombardier were also anxious about their markets.

The agricultural community, which weathered the foot-and-mouth crisis of 2001, lost its EU subsidies but were promised a new scheme to manage the land more sustainably. Since then, loss of funding has had an impact on the numbers of sheep put out to graze in an area known for its moors and dry stone walls.

Traditional Landscapes and Skills with New Uses

There are approximately 26,000 miles of dry stone wall in the Peak District. The oldest, irregular walls have marked boundaries for thousands of years. Others, usually the regular rectangular field systems, indicate enclosure by wealthy landowners during the eighteenth century by Act of Parliament. These walls were often built by Irish navvies seeking work outside famine-torn Ireland using their own regional techniques.

Farmers still maintain boundary and field walls using traditional methods, but today men and women, including champion wallers Gordon and Jason Wilton, who work with artist and sculptor Andy Goldsworthy, export Derbyshire dry stone walling skills around the world, including New York and Hawaii, to create sculptural walls that have their roots in Derbyshire's heritage.

The walls are not the only thing about the landscape to be put to new uses. The Peak District is covered by layers of peat up to 3m deep in places. It was laid down about 3,000 years ago. Twenty million tonnes of carbon are stored there, making it the UK's largest carbon store. Healthy peatlands can store even more peat, but damage caused by erosion, burning and overgrazing means that in some areas the loss of peat is adding to the problem of global warming as carbon dioxide is returned to the atmosphere. The National Trust, which owns approximately 46,950 acres of the Peak District, works with the Peak Park to reverse the losses of earlier times to slow carbon emissions.

WATER, WATER EVERYWHERE

In August 2019, much of Whaley Bridge was evacuated after heavy rains caused damage to a dam wall holding back Toddbrook Reservoir above the town, which began to crumble. An RAF Chinook was part of the operation to repair the structure.

The rain continued in October, and in November Derbyshire experienced twenty-four hours of heavy rainfall that resulted in already full rivers bursting their banks and landslips, leading to the closure of railway lines and more than 100 roads. There was one fatality near Matlock. Storm Atiyah caused gales in December, Storm Brendan bought more rain in January, and Storm Ciara swept across the county on 9 February, bringing gales and heavy downpours. The River Trent burst its banks at Swarkestone; there was a landslide between Cromford and Lea Bridge. At Matlock, the River Derwent broke its banks and flooded the town. It was the wettest February on record. Derbyshire County Council stated that the floods caused £20 million damage to the county's roads.

COVID-19

By the end of March 2020, Derby saw its first confirmed case of coronavirus. People went about their lives as usual until schools and pubs across Derbyshire closed on 20 March 2020 to prevent the spread of the virus. On 23 March, the nation was told to stay at home. It was the first of three national lockdowns. In Derbyshire, a lot changed in a short time.

Derby County games went ahead in their Pride Park stadium, but there were no supporters in the stands and the streets of Derbyshire's towns were deserted. As the weather heated up, the county made national news when local authorities decided to dye the Blue Lagoon near Buxton black to deter people from swimming in its toxic waters. In Swadlincote, a street went viral on social media when neighbours joined together, at a distance, to perform a dance to the 1980s song Footloose. Edale was voted as one of the best places in the country to live, not only because of its beautiful scenery but also because of its community spirit. Derbyshire County Council launched a campaign called Derbyshire Spirit that aimed to celebrate the county's key workers as well as the way in which communities helped one another during unpresented times. It recognised that the true spirit of the county, in every hamlet, village and town, was its people, as they looked out for one another.

A Platinum Jubilee fit for a Queen

As Derbyshire emerged into a post-Covid world, it prepared to celebrate the 70th anniversary of the late Queen Elizabeth II's accession to the throne in 1953 with a four-day bank holiday at the beginning of June 2022. Beacons were lit; street parties, picnics and parades were held across the county, resulting in the closure of 160 roads that weekend; trees were planted across the region to form part of the Queen's Green Canopy; and many of the Peak District's well dressings that year paid their respects to the queen using pictures celebrating her reign made from seeds and flower petals pressed into boards of clay, including one at Hartington that depicted Paddington Bear.

Conclusion

From stone circles to the Romans baths at Buxton, to the keep at Castleton and Bess of Hardwick's building projects, the technological developments and social upheaval of the Industrial Revolution recognised by Derbyshire UNESCO World Heritage sites, the mass trespass of Kinder Scout and the founding of Britain's first National Park, Derbyshire's people, down-to-earth and practical folk, are grounded in the county's landscape and mineral wealth. They remain independent minded, enterprising and at the forefront of pioneering transformations, as they have for more than a thousand years. There's no telling what Derbyshire might do next!

BIBLIOGRAPHY

JOURNALS AND PERIODICALS

Derbyshire Archaeological Journal, 1879–2023
Derbyshire Life
Derbyshire Times
Nottingham and Derbyshire Notes and Queries, 1892–98

BOOKS

Appleby, John C., and Dalton, Paul (eds.), *Outlaws in Medieval and Early Modern England: Crime, Government and Society, c.1066–c.1600* (Abingdon: Ashgate Publishing, 2009)

Bailey, Stephen, *The Old Roads of Derbyshire: Walking into History: The Portway and Beyond* (Kibworth: Matador, 2019)

Barnatt, John, *Arbor Low: A Guide to the Monuments* (Bakewell: Peak National Park, 1996)

Barnatt, John, *Reading the Peak District Landscape* (Swindon: Historic England, 2019)

Bevan, Bill, *Ancient Peakland* (Wellington: Halsgrove, 2007)

Breeze, A., 'The Name of Lutudarum, Derbyshire', *Britannia*, Volume 33 (Cambridge: Cambridge University Press, 2011) pp.266–68

Castor, Helen, '"Walter Blount was gone to serve traytors": the sack of Elvaston and the Politics of the North Midlands in 1454', The Midland History Prize Essay, *Midland History*, Vol. 19, 1994, Issue 1, pp.21–39

Childs, Joy, *A History of Derbyshire* (Chichester: Phillimore & Co., 1987)

Craven, Maxwell, *Derby, An Illustrated History* (Derby: Breedon Books, 1988)

Dalton, Paul, 'The Outlaw Hereward "the Wake": His Companions and Enemies', in Appleby, John C. and Dalton, Paul, *Outlaws in Medieval and Early England: Crime Government and Society, c.1066–c.1600*, (London: Routledge, 2009) pp.7–36

Defoe, Daniel, *A Tour Thro' the Whole Island of Great Britain*, Vol. II (London: 1724; reprinted London: Penguin Books, 2005)

Dodds, Ben and Britnell, Richard (eds), *Agriculture and Rural Society after the Black Death*, Volume 6 (Hatfield: University of Hertfordshire Press, 2008)

Emery, Anthony, *Great Medieval Houses of England and Wales, 1300–1500: Volume 2, East Anglia, Central England and Wales*, (Cambridge: Cambridge University Press, 1996)

Fearnehough, David, *Derbyshire Extremes* (Stroud: Amberley Publishing, 2010)

Frost, Warwick and Hall, Michael (eds), *Tourism and National Parks: International Perspectives on Development, History and Change* (London: Routledge, 2009)

Hall, George, *The History of Chesterfield: With Particulars of the Hamlets* (London: Wittaker and Co, 1839)

Hattersley, Roy, *The Devonshires: The Story of a Family and a Nation* (London: Vintage Books, 2014)

Jewell, Helen M., *The North–South Divide: The Origins of Northern Consciousness in England* (Manchester: Manchester University Press, 1994)

Lovell, Mary S., *Bess of Hardwick, First Lady of Chatsworth* (London: Abacus, 2005)

Lysons, Daniel, and Lysons, Samuel, *Magna Britannia, Volume 5: Derbyshire* (London: T.Cadell and W. Davies, 1817)

Mee, Arthur, *The King's England – Derbyshire* (London: Hodder and Stoughton, 1969)

Morgan, Philip (ed.) and Wood, Sara (trans.), *Domesday Book: Derbyshire* (Chichester: Philimore, 1978)

Nigota, Joseph, 'Vernon Family', *Oxford Dictionary of National Biography* (online edition) (Oxford: Oxford University Press, 2004)

O Brien, William, *Prehistoric Copper Mining in Europe 5500–500BC* (Oxford: OUP, 2015)

Page, William (ed.), *A History of the County of Derby*, Volumes 1 and 2 (London: Victoria County History, 1905 and 1907)

Patterson, Mark, *Roman Derbyshire* (Nottingham: Five Leaves Publications, 2016)

Peak District National Park Authority, Fact Sheet 4, *Quarrying and mineral extraction in the Peak District National Park*

Peak District National Park Authority, *The State of the Park Report* (2021)

Pearson, John, *The Serpent and the Stag* (New York: William Abrahams, 1983)

Pevsner, Nikolaus, revised by Williamson, Elizabeth, *The Buildings of England: Derbyshire* (London: Penguin, 2000)

Pick, Christopher (ed.), Savage, Anne (trans.), *The Anglo-Saxon Chronicles* (Godalming: CLB Publishing, 1995)

Riden, Philip, *A History of Chesterfield, Tudor and Stuart Chesterfield*, Volume 2, Parts 1 and 2 (Chesterfield: Borough of Chesterfield, 1984)

Scollins, Richard and Titford, John, *Ey Up Mi Duck! Dialect of Derbyshire and the East Midlands* (Newbury: Countryside Books, 2000)

Sidebottom, Phil, *Pecsaentna: People of the Anglo-Saxon Peak District* (Oxford: Oxbow Books, 2020)

Smith, Michael E., *Industrial Derbyshire* (Derby: Breedon Books, 2008)

Stevens, John, *England's Last Revolution Pentrich 1817* (Hartington: Moorland Publishing Company, 1977)

Stone, Brian, *Derbyshire in the Civil War* (Cromford: Scarthin Books, 1992)

Turbutt, Gladwyn, *A History of Derbyshire*, Volumes 1–4 (Cardiff: Merton Priory Press, 1999)

Williams, Thomas, *Viking Britain: A History* (London: William Collins, 2017)

Wiltshire, Mary and Woore, Sue, *Monastic Granges in Derbyshire* (Ashbourne: W&WP, 2019)

Wright, Susan M., *The Derbyshire Gentry of the Fifteenth Century* (Walton: Derbyshire Record Society, 1983)

Yeatman, John Pym, Sitwell, George and Foljambe, Cecil, *The Feudal History of the County of Derby*, Volume 1 (London: Bemrose and Sons, 1886)

WEBSITES

www.derbymuseums.org

www.derbyshire.gov.uk

Derbyshire Historic Environment Record (HER) her.derbyshire.gov.uk

www.peakdistrict.gov.uk

INDEX